MIDCENTURY COCKTAILS

Midcentury Cocktails

HISTORY, LORE, AND RECIPES FROM AMERICA'S ATOMIC AGE

Cecelia Tichi

WASHINGTON MEWS BOOKS

An Imprint of

NEW YORK UNIVERSITY PRESS

New York

NEW YORK UNIVERSITY PRESS
New York
www.nyupress.org

References to Internet websites (URLs) were accurate at the time of writing. Neither the author nor New York University Press is responsible for URLs that may have expired or changed since the manuscript was prepared.

Please contact the Library of Congress for Cataloging-in-Publication data.
ISBN: 9781479816651 (hardback)
ISBN: 9781479816699 (library ebook)
ISBN: 9781479816668 (consumer ebook)

New York University Press books are printed on acid-free paper, and their binding materials are chosen for strength and durability. We strive to use environmentally responsible suppliers and materials to the greatest extent possible in publishing our books.

Manufactured in the United States of America

10 9 8 7 6 5 4 3 2 1

Also available as an ebook

CONTENTS

Introduction: *Midcentury Living from A to Z* 1

1. On the Road(s) 11
2. Barbizonia 26
3. Gray Flannel Suits 37
4. The Bar Car 44
5. *Le weekend* 48
6. Pulitzers versus Potboilers 58
7. Bunnies and Playboys 69
8. Jet Set 80
9. Tiki Time 94
10. Bachelor Pads 108
11. Breakfasting at Tiffany's 120
12. *Islands in the Stream* 127
13. Green Booking 135
14. Atoms for Peace 143

Acknowledgments 149
Bibliography 151
Index 157
About the Author 159

INTRODUCTION

Midcentury Living from A to Z

America at midcentury was a nation on the move, taking to wings and wheels along the new interstate highways and in passenger jets that soared to thirty thousand feet above the earth. Centered in the presidency of General Dwight Eisenhower (1953–61), the period that stretched from the post-WWII baby boom years into the increasingly volatile mid-1960s promised affordable homes for those who never had dreamed of owning property and an array of gleaming appliances to fill them. The country doubled down on two-car garages and driveways boasting recent models of the Chevy Brookwood or Ford Country Squire station wagon, which sported the flaring tail fins that Detroit automakers styled after Space Age rockets. New suburban shopping malls offered a vast array of consumer goods and "quick & easy" meals gave homemakers a break from the hot kitchen. Medical science advanced with antibiotic wonder drugs, and Dr. Jonas Salk developed a vaccine that prevented the terrifying summertime scourge of poliomyelitis. The television console dominated the living room, like an electronic hearth, and in December 1953 RCA turned the black-and-white image into "Living Color." As tourism flourished at home and abroad, the country quaffed new cocktails that reflected the nation's modern, informal lifestyle and worldly outlook. The old days of Prohibition, the Depression, and WWII had spurred flagrant hard drinking, but the hallmark of the new era was purely social, the pleasure of an evening imbibing in mixed company, a middle-class idea of sophisticated leisure.

The images conjured up by the Madmen of Madison Avenue set the tone for convivial libations. Print ads showed suburban sophisticates—women in high heels and cocktail dresses, men in coat-and-tie or tuxedos—enjoying their drinks at leisure. In one promotion, a smiling woman returns from shopping with gift-wrapped bundles in each arm and confides, "We all know I will use any excuse to have a glamorous cocktail . . . Oh, it's the weekend, I guess I need to have a cocktail . . . Oh, it's the full moon. Cocktail time!" She pauses, then, "You say it's the second Tuesday of the Month? Pour me a glass!" "I don't normally have dessert after dinner," she adds, "but a cocktail . . ." The right scotch might attract and keep good friends. Seagram's V.O. promised "the world's lightest high-ball" for ladies, while on principle "any drink worth making is worth making more." The ubiquitous midcentury accolade "labor-saving" applied also to the premixed drinks that surged in popularity. One company boasted of its "Five Kinds" of drinks: Dry Martini, Manhattan, Old Fashioned, Side Car, Daiquiri. "The finest liquors that money can buy are in the bottle . . . just pour over ice."

American cities remained hubs of commerce and nighttime entertainment. Three-Martini business lunches and dinners could precede late-night drinks at clubs like New York's El Morocco or 21. After 1960, Playboy Clubs mushroomed in cities coast to coast and in hubs worldwide, and Hugh Hefner (b. 1926) oversaw the sultry "Bunnies" who served food and drinks to members and guests. High-rise city apartments also became cocktail oases, like the Manhattan "tower hotel" where a young bachelor in John Cheever's story "The Cure" goes "way, way, way up" to a terrace cocktail party in search of "a pretty girl in new shoes." He might just as well have prowled the lobby of the Barbizon, the New York hotel that since 1928 had been a home for ambitious young women in search of exciting careers. The Barbizon served no alcohol, but young female residents, some who became distinguished in the arts, tippled in nearby cafés or in bachelors' apartments.

As the census ballooned from 132 million in 1940 to 179 million in 1960, suburbs grew around American cities. On New York's Long Island, Brooklyn-born contractor William Levitt (b. 1907) mass-produced 10,600 fully furnished houses by 1950, most financed by low-cost veterans' (GI) loans, that held out the promise of "A New Way of Life." "I'll never forget those years," exclaimed one vet. "You talk about dreams . . . we were pioneers." The crabgrass frontier stretched from the modest Levittown lots (60-by-100 feet), where backyard grills fired up alongside coolers of plentiful cold brews ("If you like beer, you'll love Schlitz!"). Levittown's blue-collar "Joe Six-Pack," who clocked in for a shift at the plant or garage and proudly donned his satin bowling shirt to roll strikes and spares on weekends, would seldom, if ever, join the new upscale cocktail cohort. Nor would his wife, who might join girlfriends at the bingo hall on weekday nights and try her luck. She and her hubby might enjoy a highball now and then, but the "church key" that opened beer cans was much oftener in use than the corkscrew. The brewers' newer pop-top meant convenience, never mind the hoity-toity folks who planted swizzle sticks in fancy mixed drinks.

In the wealthier leafy exurbs, all the while, upper-middle-class executives in their gray flannel suits unwound at day's end with drinks in the boisterous bar cars of the commuter lines, which social critic A. C. Spectorsky dubbed "a decorous rolling saloon, catering to the wealthy sedate." Beyond the urban hubbub, bourbon or scotch quenched thirst on the rails, and Martinis awaited the exurbanite at his lushly landscaped home in Connecticut or Westchester. Upscale suburban cocktail parties like those in John Cheever's stories punctuated the weekends, where, according to advertising guru David Ogilvy, mixed Gin and Tonics guaranteed "a feeling of good taste." Cigarettes were ubiquitous at home and in the office.

The suburban "new way of life" reflected the country's cherished (and often sanitized) past. Suburban home styles harkened to an earlier America with two-story colonials, Cape Cod cottages, and ranch houses from the Old West. On television models branded the Revere and the Plymouth, a morally rigorous Old West was dramatized weekly in *Gunsmoke*, which debuted in 1955, and the previous year Disney had launched the adventures of Davy Crockett. Costumed in fringed buckskins and wielding a hunting knife and musket, dauntless Davy (actor Fess Parker) sparked a mania for caps made of racoon fur or the new synthetics. "The Ballad of Davy Crockett" became a 1950s radio hit, and Tennessee's Senator Estes Kefauver donned a signature coonskin cap in the era when men's hats were not optional. (The Davey [*sic*] Crockett cocktail, a concoction of blue curaçao, peach schnapps, and orange juice, was to memorialize the show and its hero in years to come.)

As TV promised to make the viewer an "armchair Columbus," road trips to "See America First" vied with tantalizing visions of offshore travel. On the wildly popular sitcom *I Love Lucy*, the Cuban bandleader Desi Arnaz evoked the romance of the island nation some ninety miles from US shores. Americans had vacationed in Cuba since the 1910s, but midcentury prosperity swelled the numbers who alighted in Havana for casino gambling, risqué floorshows, and Bacardi rum cocktails such as the Cuba Libre or Mojito. The famous writer "Papa" Ernest Hemingway had taken up residence on the island at a farm-like *finca* outside of Havana but ventured into the city to enjoy frozen Daiquiris at the Floridita restaurant. (Backcountry skirmishes hinted at unrest, but Fidel Castro became a boldface name only at the end of 1958, when the Cuban government was toppled.)

Other islands and islanders beckoned, especially the alluring beaches of the French- and British-ruled Caribbean. Unaffordable during the Depression and unthinkable through WWII, interest in travel to the nearby islands surged to the soundtrack of Harry Belafonte's million-selling 1956 album *Calypso*. Like Cuba, the islands had supplied the States with illicit liquor and wines during Prohibition in the 1920s and now offered American tourists the Jamaican Breeze, the Dark and Stormy, and the Appleton Mule, among other libations. At the same time, genial TV host Arthur Godfrey donned short-sleeved aloha shirts and floral leis while strumming a ukulele and singing songs of the Hawaiian Islands, which became the fiftieth state of the Union in 1959. The Royal Hawaiian Hotel's Mai-Tai Bar dispensed Blue Hawaiian and Mai-Tai cocktails while patrons eyed surfers and outrigger canoes plying the curling waves along famed Waikiki beach. Piquing interest in the Polynesian islands, the Rodgers and Hammerstein musical *South Pacific*, starring Mary Martin and Ezio Pinza, opened on Broadway in April 1949. The following year, the bestseller list featured *Kon-Tiki*, the Norwegian Thor Heyerdahl's account of rafting across the Pacific from Peru to Tahiti. Cocktail lounges and restaurants imported "Polynesia" to the mainland with bamboo chairs, palms, and "tiki" drinks, among them the Shark's Tooth, the Wahini, and the Aku Aku.

At home, prosperity had failed to inoculate the country against fears that our own government had become a hive of communists. In 1954, Senator Joseph McCarthy (b. 1908), a Wisconsin Republican, waved phony documents before the TV cameras and swore they contained the names of treasonous Communist Party members. McCarthyism ultimately collapsed with the exposure of his lies and fabricated evidence, although not before careers and lives were damaged.

The suburbs and remote exurbs exposed a social hierarchy that most Americans claimed did not exist. To the contrary, class-based social layering became pervasive, insisted sociologist C. Wright Mills's *White Collar* (1951) and bestselling Vance Packard's *The Status Seekers* (1959). Their findings showed Americans colonized the suburbs in stratified classes based on jobs, education, religion, foods, sports, and so on, with income just one of several factors defining status. Within suburban households of every class, a "generation gap" erupted when teens' record players throbbed with the 45-rpm rock 'n' roll music that parents feared promoted juvenile delinquency. Rock music burst racial boundaries as teens danced the Twist to Chubby Checker and sang along to Buddy Holly, Chuck Berry, and Jerry Lee (the "Killer") Lewis. Most worrisome to parents was the hip-gyrating

"King," Elvis Presley, who brought sex to the child-rearing equation. A teetotaler who favored Coca-Cola, Elvis nonetheless inspired dread that the younger generation might be lost to lust and crime.

America's suburban paradise had excluded Blacks and other people of color from its bounty, including honorably discharged veterans who were denied home ownership opportunities. As a Jew, William Levitt knew how damaging bias could be, but by 1960 "not a single one of the Long Island Levittown's 82,000 residents was Black." Whites-only suburbs surrounded "a nationwide system of urban ghettos," Richard Rothstein points out in *The Color of Law*. TV news cameras recorded the struggles of nicely dressed young men and women forbidden to enjoy a sandwich and a Coke at a lunch counter, and in 1954, the US Supreme Court unanimously ruled in the case of *Brown v. Board of Education of Topeka* that "in the field of public education the doctrine of 'separate but equal' has no place" and ordered "a prompt and reasonable start toward full compliance."

For Black motorists, traveling by car afforded a kind of freedom not found on segregated public transport. Resourceful drivers relied on *The Negro Motorist Green Book*, a directory of hospitable services, restaurants, lodgings, and entertainment spots welcoming African Americans in cities and towns nationwide and on visits home by families who had traveled "up south" during the Great Migration. In his guide, Victor Green provided useful information on everything from the best car models, from the economical Chevrolet to the "luxurious" Pontiac and "DeLuxe" Oldsmobile and Cadillac, to nightspots like Detroit's Flame, Chicago's Club De Lisa, or LA's Club Alabam, which featured cocktails made famous by the celebrated Gilded Age Black mixologist Tom Bullock's *Ideal Bartender* (1917) and other drinks and live jazz for locals and travelers. White suburban women also found themselves marooned in the "Consumers' Republic," as historian Lizabeth Cohen calls it. Few knew that the US government and the editors of women's favorite monthly magazines had collaborated to ensure jobs for returning WWII vets by luring "Rosie the Riveter" and her college-educated sister to homes in the postwar suburbs. The *Ladies' Home Journal* and other magazines depicted heroic wartime women workers yearning to quit their jobs and embrace full-time domestic life. Tributes to "Occupation: Housewife" appeared throughout the midcentury years, and satirist Russel Lynes spoofed the suburban mother whose household "resembles a one room school at recess—children everywhere." Betty Friedan exploded the kitchen and romper-room myth with 1963's blockbuster bestseller *The Feminine Mystique*, an indictment of the illusion of domestic "feminine fulfillment."

Beneath the midcentury sheen, domestic social and political conflict roiled, as did international affairs. The Cold War, ushered in when Russia detonated its own nuclear device in 1949, confirmed that America did not uniquely possess nuclear secrets, and the space race hastened when the Soviet Union sent its *Sputnik* satellite orbiting the earth in 1957. Seven years earlier, in 1950, a war-weary America had returned to the battlefield on the Korean peninsula, pitting US troops against North Koreans and their Chinese reinforcements who had violated a WWII agreement to divide the peninsula at the 38th parallel. The fighting dragged on until the truce of July 1953, though no peace agreement was ever signed.

Changing fashion and evolving politics turned the page on midcentury favorites when an unfamiliar East Asian country drew fretful public attention. The US military advisors posted to South Vietnam in the mid-1960s augured American combat in faraway jungles, and a military draft loomed on the horizon. Recreational drugs, notably the psychedelic LSD (lysergic acid diethylamide), provided their own brand of mood adjustment in some quarters, as did hashish, peyote, and marijuana. Women gathered in consciousness-raising groups to discuss the dynamics of gender based on personal experiences, and their liberating feminist campaigns soon followed, marked by public demonstrations and a myth of "bra burning." The vibrant, all-too-short presidency of John Fitzgerald Kennedy ended tragically in November 1963, yielding to President Lyndon B. Johnson's escalating deployments and the bellicose policies of Richard Milhous Nixon.

For now, an admiring world still welcomed Levi's jeans, jazz music, and Hollywood movies. At home, the cocktail classics prevailed—the Martini, Manhattan, and Old Fashioned, each endlessly tweaked by midcentury bartenders at home and abroad. The "Atomic Age" itself may have unleashed appetites for alcohol, as historian Elaine Tyler May has found, for it briefly freed imbibers from Cold War angst. Every bartender and liquor dealer saw scotch whisky reach new heights of prestige and popularity in these years, and the newest bar guides kept pace with the times. *A Guide to Pink Elephants* stood side by side with *Summer Drinks, Quintessential Cocktails, The Sheraton Waikiki Tiki Restaurant Bar*, and a standby edition of 1955, *Old Mr. Boston's Official Bartender's Guide*.

(Even as Americans learned to "duck and cover," the "bomb" inspired a few new concoctions for the Age of the Atom.) Together, they provide a kind of time capsule from the fifties, ready to open for revival in this twenty-first century when the midcentury moment flares once again.

1

ON THE ROAD(S)

Hit the road, Jack.
—Percy Mayfield, 1960

Songwriter Percy Mayfield's anthem blared from radios and vinyl recordings in four big beats—"Hit the Road Jack"—stirring the nation to get a move on, *now!* Popularized by hitmaker Ray Charles, the midcentury musical mandate tapped the country's "restless temper," which was noticed as far back as 1831 by the astute French traveler Alexis de Tocqueville, who added, "Once they migrate, they circulate." Motor magnate Henry Ford II (b. 1917) updated Tocqueville in 1956: "We Americans always like plenty of elbow room—freedom to come and go as we please in this big country of ours." In these years, America eagerly sped along the multilane divided highways of the new interstate system. Licensed to drive, the Jacks and Jackies took the wheel, cranked up the radio, and hit the road to meet their futures. Doing so, they evoked the mythic road embedded in the nation's psyche from colonial days, for the road meant freedom, escape, ambition, and fresh starts in a country that prized starting over.

The American road had beckoned from a mind's-eye view when Virginia's Thomas Jefferson gazed westward across the Blue Ridge Mountains in the 1770s and mused that the country's future lay in vast terrain that he was to claim one day for the new United States. As chief executive in 1803,

President Jefferson negotiated the purchase of nearly one million (828,000) square miles from France for the sum of $15 million. The Louisiana Purchase meshed with the vision Jefferson had recorded on his plantation two decades earlier in *Notes on the State of Virginia*, when he surveyed the distance through a mountain cleft and wrote, "That way the road happens actually to lead."

Poet Walt Whitman recharged the visionary road when he penned "The Song of the Open Road" (1856–82), a paean to wanderlust beyond the city streets and curbstones. "Afoot and light-hearted," Walt proclaimed, "I take to the open road. . . . O public road. . . . O highway. . . . Allons! The road is before us!" The poet swore his "own feet have tried it well," but footsore pioneers in covered wagons mired in mud eagerly gave way to the railroad and the "horseless carriages" of the early twentieth century, although these, too, foundered on roads barely worthy of the name. The Good Roads movement promoted pavement from the late 1870s, and a transcontinental highway—the Lincoln Highway—was dedicated in 1913 to inaugurate coast-to-coast travel in the Age of the Automobile.

Aspiration had outpaced function, for the map that smoothly routed autos from New York City's Times Square to San Francisco's Lincoln Park bore little relation to motorists' realities. Theoretically, the Lincoln Highway opened for such 1910s models as the Overland, the Hupmobile, the Paige Detroit Challenger, the Knox Roadster, the Reeves Octoauto (called Big Brother for its eight wheels), and numerous others, including the Ford Model T ("Tin Lizzie") that Henry Ford had produced for America's roads from 1908. The Lizzies, no less than the bygone brands, were no match for quagmires that earned farmers with plow horses tidy sums towing road-sters and touring cars from the muck.

The Lincoln Highway underwent its severest trial while of-fering a nascent hint of the future Interstate Highway System when, to promote the Good Roads campaign in postwar 1919, a US military convoy left Washington, DC, on July 7, bound for California with some eighty vehicles transporting 258 enlisted men and twenty-four officers, including Lieutenant Colonel Dwight D. Eisenhower. For the next two months, as historian Pete Davies recounts, the convoy coped with me-chanical mishaps and impossible road conditions. Among other trials, the road warriors chronicled burned-out engine bearings, overheated engines, loss of oil, failing brakes, a bro-ken piston, and jammed carburetors. Their vehicles skidded, careened, crashed, and sank in "mud, mud, everlasting mud," or got tapped in "ruts, chuckholes, quicksand, feeble bridges, and ramshackle detours." Over the Sierras, the road became "a twisting ribbon of sand and broken stone precariously cut into the mountains over sheer drops . . . of two thousand feet." In California at long last in September, the convoy was cheered as the "conqueror of every obstacle presented . . . an unprecedented argument for national highways."

By post-WWI, US automobile ownership had reached nearly 6.7 million vehicles, while the tires they ran on rolled from Goodyear, Goodrich, Firestone, and other Akron, Ohio, factories that made certain the rubber met the road. Thirty-seven years later, President Eisenhower signed into law the biggest civil-engineering project in world history. It would, as he claimed, "change the face of America." The Federal Aid Highway Act of 1956 authorized "$25 billion for twelve years to accelerate construction of a National System of Interstate and Defense Highways." A three-cent fuel tax (up from two cents) satisfied motorists and businesses that were promised "better and safer roads" with easy access on- and off-ramps that let motorists glide at high speeds without the annoyance of intersections or traffic lights. Some forty-one thousand miles of concrete would be poured in the years to come and encircle the "major metropolitan areas of forty-three states and the District of Columbia."

The newly built interstates partnered, in effect, with "Motor City" Detroit. In 1956, the Ford Motor Company published *Freedom of the American Road*, the same year that NBC debuted TV's *The Dinah Shore Chevy Show*, starring big-band singer Dinah Shore (b. 1916), whose theme song invited vacationers to "See the U.S.A. in your Chevrolet . . . America is asking you to call!" Across the nation, interchanges became oases of food, fuel, and lodgings as familiar logos beckoned motorists to Holiday Inn, Howard Johnson's, Stuckey's, McDonald's, and the gas pumps of Esso, Texaco, Gulf, and other midcentury refiners of petroleum.

The two-lane US blacktops seemed fated to fade away. Storied routes such as US 1 along the East Coast and the cross-country US 66 seemed best left to outdated AAA maps and elders' memories of favorite diners or mom-and-pop tourist courts in small cities and towns bypassed by the interstates.

The older roadways resurged, instead, in bestselling travelogues by Jack Kerouac (b. 1922) and John Steinbeck (b. 1902), both recording ample alcoholic lubrication in memoirs that became midcentury classics. Kerouac and Steinbeck reprised the older American asphalt as the space where gas-powered movement gave rise to the freest "thinking" untethered from settled "thought." Kerouac's *On the Road* (1957) and Steinbeck's *Travels with Charley: In Search of America* (1962) took readers along the blind curves, switchbacks, and straightaways that promised driver and passenger the quintessential American experience while engines revved and "bonus" encounters on byways gave rise to revelations, often aided by libations of the brewery or distillery. For both writers, "on the road" paradoxically meant off-road—to be precise, off the interstates.

Born one generation before the Interstate Highway System, Jack Kerouac necessarily ventured on two-lane blacktops from 1947 to 1950, although *On the Road* saw midcentury print only after one publisher, Viking, bet on a book that promoted sex, drugs, beer, liquor, and interracial camaraderie in jazz clubs. In the midcentury moment, Kerouac became a spokesman for "the beat generation . . . hip without being slick."

The "darkly intense, handsome" French Canadian Kerouac was baptized Jean-Louis Lebris de Kerouac and raised in a working-class family in industrial Lowell, Massachusetts. Recruited for football at Columbia University, he was sidelined by a broken leg, lost his scholarship, and took odd jobs around New York. Joining the Navy, he ended up being discharged after pleading he was "too much of a nut, and a man of letters." Stints in the merchant marine followed, and a brief marriage to Edie Parker, annulled by mutual consent. Kerouac formed friendships with aspirant writers Allen Ginsberg and William Burroughs, and with free-spirited "blood brother" Neal Cassady, who was memorialized in *On the Road* in which Kerouac becomes the fictional Sal Paradise and Cassady the character named Dean Moriarty.

The legend persists of a Benzedrine-fueled Jack Kerouac writing *On the Road* in a nonstop marathon at a typewriter rigged with paper scrolling forth as the author spontaneously produced an American literary classic that went nonstop to the publisher. Kerouac did rely on Benzedrine (and experimented with a roll of taped shelf paper), but biographer Ann Charters traces a two-year process of drafting and revising, especially under the guidance of Viking's Malcolm Cowley, who urged that fits and starts of the narrative—and the travels—be unified for concision and flow. A long effort of cutting and reworking underpinned the bestseller that burst "overnight" in a chronicle of hitchhiking, Greyhound bus rides, jalopies, and a Cadillac.

Kerouac headed "West to his future," anticipating the circa 1910 American barrooms "where men went to meet after work" at a "long counter, brass rails, spittoons, player piano for music, a few mirrors, and barrels of whisky for ten cents a shot together with barrels of beer at five cents a mug." Instead, Kerouac found himself drinking with "whole families" in countless "crossroads saloons" where the "kids eat popcorn and chips and play in back," though elsewhere he faced his share of "hostile bartenders," "anxious owners," and the "deadly silence when a stranger walks in."

Whiskey mapped Kerouac's cross-country "pilgrimage." A quart of "Old Grandad bourbon" merits mention, but the beer quaffed in Iowa became the prelude to "rotgut" swigged "in the wild, lyrical, drizzling air of Nebraska," where good fellows chipped in to buy a "fifth" in a "whisky store" and passed the bottle around before the vast rangelands that made Kerouac feel "like an arrow that could shoot out all the way." Wyoming loomed ahead, a state with cowboys, dude ranch tourists, ranchers, oilmen, and rounds of "Scotches" to treat saloon patrons, though Kerouac ordered cheap beer for himself and his partner of the moment, Montana Slim.

The Colorado Rockies offered a summertime opera festival (*Fidelio*), a bucket of brews, barhopping, dancing, and a vision of "jackpines in the moon" and "the ghosts of old miners," while the Utah desert quickened with "mad drunken Americans in the mighty land . . . on the roof of America" (but "all we could do was yell"). Farther west, San Francisco presented "a great riot of construction work" and a bar that served a whiskey-and-port-wine medley called a "Winespodiodi." Southern California awaited with "stars that are lost in the brown halo of the huge desert encampment that LA really is," the city air wafting "marijuana . . . chili beans and beer." "Everybody had come to make the movies" in Hollywood, he found, especially the "long-haired hipsters straight off Route 66 from New York." Tempted to linger in Tinsel Town, the self-styled pilgrim followed the road eastward to New Orleans where the "Mississippi River poured down," and the French Quarter's "dull bars" nonetheless served a fellow's girfriend "goofballs [barbiturates], benny [Benzedrine], liquor," and a "martini."

Dipping south into Mexico, Kerouac and Cassady (and their hitchhiker) quaffed "bottles of cold beer—*cerveza* was the name," and they found Mexico City filled with "thousands of hipsters in floppy straw hats . . . selling crucifixes and weed," plus a favorite drink—"coffee mixed with rum and nutmeg"— served in "closet-size bars stuck in adobe walls." Back in New York's Times Square, he "had traveled eight thousand miles around the American continent" to come back to "millions and millions hustling forever for a buck." His conclusion became Kerouac's most-quoted line: "The road is life."

Streaking to sales that would exceed three million copies, *On the Road* was followed by *Travels with Charley* and a 1962 Nobel Prize in literature for author John Steinbeck, who had christened US Route 66 "the Mother Road" in his bestselling *The Grapes of Wrath* (1939), the saga of a Depression- and Dust Bowl–era family migrating west in a jalopy bound for California, Steinbeck's home state. Like Kerouac, Steinbeck had left college without a degree and worked odd jobs, construction, and carpentry, and he, like Kerouac, served a stint in the merchant marine. The Golden State's Monterey and the Salinas Valley were featured in Steinbeck's *Tortilla Flat*, *Of Mice and Men*, and *East of Eden*, all drawn from the author's hardscrabble years when he managed to pen pieces he sold to major US magazines, including the *Saturday Evening Post* and *Collier's*, gradually building his literary reputation and livelihood.

Despite a long and successful literary career filled with international travel, the fifty-eight-year-old Steinbeck feared he had "lost the flavor and taste and sound" of America. The solo road trip, he trusted, would offer "a re-knowledge" of the country, "its speeches, its views, its attitudes and its changes." Driving a customized Ford pickup truck outfitted like a modern-day RV, Steinbeck gassed up and hit the road in autumn 1960, planning to circle the country from New England into the Midwest, then to the Pacific Northwest and south into California, returning east through the southwest and up the East Coast to his New York home. He would travel incognito, lest his name as a public figure warp his American experience, and he would check into motels now and then for a good night's sleep and a shower. His wife, Elaine, agreed to meet him at strategic points, but he felt the need to "go alone . . . self-contained."

Driving the backroads, Steinbeck prepared to "hit small towns and farms and ranches, sit in bars and hamburger stands and on Sunday go to church." "If a wayfaring stranger wishes to eavesdrop on a local population," the best places would be "bars and churches." His sole companion, a "French gentleman of a poodle," was ten-year-old Charley. (Steinbeck named his truck for a horse in the novel *Don Quixote*: Rocinante.)

The first autumn afternoon in Connecticut prompted a thought: "it might be nice to invite people he met along the way . . . for a drink," so Rocinante was promptly stocked with "bourbon, scotch, gin, vermouth, vodka, a medium good brandy, aged applejack, and a case of beer," since "you never know what people will want to drink."

The *Travels* notebooks began to fill when the New Hampshire farmer who let Steinbeck park for the night requested a peek at Rocinante's interior. Over coffee fortified

with applejack's "authority," the two men discussed the day's politics (Soviet premier Nikita Khrushchev had pounded his shoe on a table at the United Nations). Another round of applejack-spiked coffee, and conversation shifted to the dearth of Americans' "peppery arguments" that had apparently become a thing of the past, a lament that lingered when Steinbeck entered Maine for the potato harvest.

"Mountains of potatoes—oceans," but Maine's potatoes were harvested by families of French Canadian "mercenaries" that Americans routinely hired for "hard and humble work." By evening, Steinbeck had invited the harvesters for "warm and friendly" conversation and "beer . . . and more beer," followed by a solemn ritual bottle of aged cognac—and "Santé"—dispensed in "plastic coffee cups, a jelly glass, a shaving mug, and several wide-mouthed pill bottles," all in the service of "the Brotherhood of Man—and the sisterhood also."

The warm fellowship ebbed in a Bangor, Maine, auto court where "everything that can be captured and held down is sealed in clear plastic." Depressed, Steinbeck was driven to vodka and a hot tub bath but revived at the sight of the Union Jack waving side by side with the Stars and Stripes at Niagara Falls and a night at "a pleasure dome" with a Scotch and Soda at the restaurant noted for its grilled beefsteak (and steak tartare for Charley).

Over dinner and Whiskey Highballs at a mobile home park, Steinbeck mused that the trailer park flouted the notion that Americans treasured their "roots." To the contrary, "Americans are a restless people, a mobile people, never satisfied with where they are." ("Every one of us, except the Negroes forced here as slaves, are descended from the restless ones.") Perhaps, Steinbeck mused, "we have overrated roots as a psychic need. Maybe . . . the deeper and more ancient is the . . . hunger to be somewhere else."

The Midwest's "huge factories and plants" gave him pause, and the truck traffic struck him "like a tidal wave . . . , a river of trucks" in air "saturated with Diesel fumes." To gain a "little time to think," Steinbeck fished lakeside with a young security guard who welcomed "a dollop of Old Granddad in the coffee," but a homesick Steinbeck looked forward to Chicago's rendezvous with wife Elaine. He did not record the drinks they enjoyed, but John Steinbeck's favorite Jack Rose cocktail would be a winning wager.

Accordion-folded paper maps flummoxed midcentury drivers, but Steinbeck had a tried-and-true technique for guidance to a North Dakota city he had imagined worthy of a motorized Marco Polo: "If you will take a map of the United States and fold it in the middle . . . and crease it sharply, right in the crease will be Fargo." The mythic Fargo of Steinbeck's boyhood fantasy now stood against the actual "traffic-troubled" and "neon-plastered" clutter of an "up-and-coming town of forty-six thousand souls." Licking his "mythological wounds" as romance butted against reality, Steinbeck opted to keep his fantastic Fargo intact in deep memory.

On to Montana, his "favorite" and his "love," but a sick Charley needed a veterinarian, and a blown tire in Oregon drove Rocinante into a muddy wallow (and prompted a Good Samaritan's rescue on a Sunday). Heading south, Steinbeck's California recalled the pioneer's "twisting mountain road," which had recently metamorphosed into a "four-lane concrete highway slashed with speeding cars." Yet San Francisco "put on a show," a "gold and white acropolis rising wave upon wave against the blue of the Pacific sky," though a family reunion in Monterey fumed with political discord, and his homecoming with former *compadres* over glasses of wine reminded him of novelist Thomas Wolfe's title *You Can't Go Home Again.*

The 1961 Thanksgiving holiday found Steinbeck in Texas voicing "an opening covey of generalities," viz., "Texas is a state of mind." "Texas is an obsession." "Texas is a nation in every sense of the word." In Texas, said Steinbeck, "businessmen wear heeled boots that never feel a stirrup, and men of great wealth who have houses in Paris and regularly shoot grouse in Scotland refer to themselves as little old country boys. . . . the 'little ol' country boy' at a symphony, the booted and blue-jeaned ranchman in Nieman-Marcus, buying Chinese jades." Invited for Thanksgiving weekend at a ranch where "the smell of money was everywhere," Steinbeck "thirstily" downed "scotch and soda," caught four trout in a private stream, dressed for dinner in "white shirt and jacket and tie," and, "after two good drinks of whisky," dined on turkey, took a walk, napped, and concluded his "Thanksgiving orgy in Texas."

The South beckoned, including New Orleans, but Steinbeck wrote, "Who has not known a journey to be over and dead before the traveler returns?" "My own journey," he reflected, "started before I left, and was over before I returned," for traveling had finally become "a gray, timeless, eventless tunnel." Steinbeck's late tunnel vision, nonetheless, was backstopped by his sharp-eyed free-thinking, soon to join *On the Road* in the canon of the American road. Both travelogues toasted a midcentury America alive and well on its backroads.

WINE-SPODIODI (À LA *ON THE ROAD*)

Ingredients:
1. 1–3 ounces whiskey
2. 3 ounces port wine

Directions:
1. Pour 1½ ounces port wine in each of 2 glasses.
2. Pour whiskey in a separate glass.
3. In order, drink: port wine, whiskey, and port wine.

MEXICAN COFFEE WITH RUM AND NUTMEG (À LA *ON THE ROAD*)

Ingredients:
1. 4 ounces hot, strong black coffee
2. 1–2 ounces rum
3. Nutmeg

Directions:
1. Pour coffee into 6-ounce heated mug or cup.
2. Add rum.
3. Grate nutmeg over surface (stir if desired).

COFFEE WITH APPLEJACK

Ingredients:
1. 4 ounces hot black coffee
2. 1 ounce applejack

Directions:
1. Pour coffee into 6-ounce heated cup or mug.
2. Add applejack and serve.

WHISKEY HIGHBALL

Ingredients:
1. 2 ounces whiskey
2. 4–6 ounces ginger ale or club soda (to taste)

Directions:
1. Put 4–5 ice cubes in 10-ounce glass.
2. Pour in whiskey.
3. Slowly add ginger ale or club soda.
4. Stir gently and serve.

COFFEE WITH OLD GRAND-DAD WHISKEY

Ingredients:
1. 4 ounces hot black coffee
2. 1–2 ounces Old Grand-Dad whiskey

Directions:
1. Pour coffee into 6-ounce heated cup or mug.
2. Add whiskey and serve.

JACK ROSE COCKTAIL

Ingredients:
1. 2 ounces applejack or brandy
2. ½ ounce grenadine

3. 1 ounce fresh lemon juice
4. 1 raspberry or apple slice for garnish

Directions:
1. Fill shaker with cubed ice.
2. Add all ingredients.
3. Shake vigorously until well chilled.
4. Strain into cocktail glass, garnish, and serve.

SCOTCH AND SODA

Ingredients:
1. 1–2 ounces scotch whisky
2. 4 ounces soda water

Directions:
1. Put 4 ice cubes into slug-bottom tumbler.
2. Add whisky.
3. Gently add soda water, stir, and serve.

2

BARBIZONIA

In New York, Fame and Fortune await you at the
Barbizon.
—Advertisement, 1950

The high-rise hotel shimmered like a fabled castle for career-minded young women eager to launch independent lives in midcentury Gotham. They came from California and the South, from Western ranches, Midwest cities, and New England towns, a mix of debutantes and shopgirls, college coeds and would-be fashion models. Wherever they had started, the Barbizon Hotel for women was their North Star in the firmament of New York City. Immersed in metropolitan social life, these young women were about to be initiated into the urban sophisticates' rite of passage—cocktails and kindred libations at receptions, luncheons, dinners, and late nights on the town.

Ambitious for successful futures, Barbizonians put their stamp on the hotel that became a New York landmark from its opening in 1928. In due course, an extraordinary group of its midcentury alumnae distinguished themselves in literature, the arts, journalism, business, and film. Among others, actors Grace Kelly, Ali McGraw, and Tippi Hedren would star in Hollywood movies, while Meg Wolitzer, Diane Johnson, and Ann Beattie succeeded in fiction, just as Gael Greene became a notable author and critic. Mary Cantwell's career in fashion

journalism dovetailed with Eileen Ford's successful modeling agency and Betsey Johnson's trademark clothing designs.
Sylvia Plath left her mark as a novelist and much-admired
poet, while Joan Didion became a foremost writer and mar-
quee public intellectual.

Barbizon alumnae also numbered among those seeking mar-
ketable clerical skills as students of the Katharine Gibbs School.
The "Katy Gibbs" dormitory occupied two Barbizon floors,
a nighttime respite from days spent mastering the typewriter
and shorthand "pothooks" to take rapid-fire dictation from
executive "madmen" and give a secretary sufficient income for
an independent livelihood. The Gibbs Girls included graduates
of elite colleges who enhanced résumés with office skills, and
they joined the scores of women who sought the advertised
"Fame and Fortune" in the seven hundred single rooms in the
twenty-three-story Gothic Revival–style building at 140 East
63rd Street on the Upper East Side of New York City.

Named for the Barbizon School, a nineteenth-century
French art movement, the hotel building featured large arched
windows at the entrance and domed windows that drew the
eye upward in a stepped-back design typical of the urban sky-
scraper. The spacious, colorful and ornate lobby with its high
ceilings, potted plants, tiling, patterned flooring, chandelier,
and upholstered furniture suggested an Italian villa, and the
mezzanine a balcony from which a *signorina* might imagine
herself serenaded (or furtively peer below to scope out the
blind date who had just walked in the door). Except for repair
technicians, all men, whether potential swains or "wolves,"
were permitted in the lobby but barred from the upper floors.

The private rooms of the Barbizon Club-Residence for
Women (its first iteration) struck newcomers as a spartan

contrast to the luxe lobby, for the narrow bed, chest of draw-
ers, small desk, and modest armchair signaled sufficiency but
hardly luxuriance. One modern feature, a radio, delighted an
early resident, the celebrated Molly Brown (Margaret Tobin
Brown, b. 1867), who survived the sinking of the *Titanic*,
gained fame on the stage, and was posthumously memorialized in the 1964 Broadway musical *The Unsinkable Molly
Brown*. From the Barbizon's early years and beyond, Molly
and her fellow residents were warned that liquor was prohib-
ited in the rooms, as were hazardous electrical "hot plates for
cheap meals . . . hair dryers, and sun lamps." Late nights were
discouraged since they hinted at "improprieties."

Residents, however, were to be uplifted and kept fit by the
hotel's amenities, including a library, art studios, musicians'
practice rooms, solarium lounge, lecture rooms, gym, and
swimming pool. Daily housekeeping service was provided, tea
served daily in late afternoons, and typewritten announce-
ments of the coming week's social events and lectures slipped
under each resident's door. By 1950, the first-floor café offered
salads, an array of sandwiches (notably the Barbizon club),
and coffee, tea, or milk—but no alcoholic drinks, though
nearby Manhattan watering holes abounded in spirited beverages. A legendary doorman, Oscar Beck (not to be confused
with head waiter Oscar Tschirky of the Waldorf-Astoria),
buoyed the young women's spirits with compliments, while
Assistant Manager Mae Sibley manned the front desk with
dour vigilance and confronted late-night arrivals with the
shaming challenge: what would your mother think?

A distinct midcentury chapter in Barbizon history began
several blocks south of the hotel in the editorial offices of
Mademoiselle magazine on Madison Avenue when Betsy

Talbot Blackwell, the editor-in-chief, faced a quandary besetting the magazine's senior editors. Since the 1940s, Blackwell
had hired a series of young women fashion editors for fixed
terms on a College Board, mined their fashion savvy, and
powerfully influenced advertisers with the data reaped from
the Board. Heading a fashion magazine geared toward "Smart
Young Women," Blackwell (b. 1905) and the other full-time
Mademoiselle editors found themselves nonetheless growing
years distant from the magazine's readership, not yet "on the
shelf," perhaps, but out of touch with the youthful fads and
fashions of the moment.

In her superb *Barbizon: The Hotel That Set Women Free*,
author Paulina Bren details the crisis moment when "a small
group of staff members were discussing what to feature for
prom-wear in the upcoming August College Issue." At the age
of twenty-five, the leading College Board editor found herself to be fashion's has-been, while Blackwell (the redoubt-
able BTB) and the senior editors, fancying themselves chic in
picture hats and pearls, realized they verged on obsolescence.
Their survival was at stake. "'That did it.' *Mademoiselle*'s
Guest Editor contest was born."

The *Mademoiselle* Guest Editor program became "the
most sought-after launching pad for girls with literary and
artistic ambitions. . . . If you were lucky enough to be one
of the chosen twenty, you were brought to New York for
the month of June to shadow senior editors at Mademoiselle
and to stay—of course!—at the Barbizon Hotel for Women."
The winning Guest Editors, however, "first had to prove
their worth as writers, artists, critical voices, and college
students" ("Write us a note *in your own handwriting* and
tell us in not less than fifty words . . . what you expect to

gain from your month at MLLE and what you think you can give the magazine"). Hired graphologists weeded out misfits, and the required photograph verified that a contestant was at least "pleasant-looking," since she would be photographed all month long, often modeling the advertisers' newest fashions.

These "Eisenhower-era Innocents," in one alum's sly term, were first marched from the Barbizon to the *Mademoiselle* offices at 575 Madison Avenue (Mad Ave), the headquarters of Street & Smith, the magazine's publisher, where notions of glamor vanished at the sight of "sparse decorations and venetian blinds," open carrels, and the few window air conditioners that proved no match for the city's hot, humid June. All the better that the flock of GEs (Blackwell's shorthand for the Guest Editors) often ranged about Manhattan for "photo shoots for the College Issue or at carefully choreographed luncheons with the magazine's advertisers."

From the luncheons into the wee hours, the GEs drank in the sights and sounds of the city and quaffed its signature drinks. "All of New York drank Manhattans and enormous martinis," and the GEs especially adored Malachy's bar, something of a Barbizon annex on Third Avenue between 63rd and 64th Streets, where the young women of *Mademoiselle* could sit at the bar and ease themselves into "the martini culture of the time." While editor Blackwell sipped a Bloody Mary at lunch and opted for scotch at 5 p.m., special events let Guest Editors slake thirsts with endless drinks served straight up or on the rocks. One such occasion was the 1955 balloon-release gala in the Hotel Astor ballroom to celebrate *Mademoiselle*'s and the fashion industry's triumphant August issue with a bar freely dispensing "Scotch and sodas." "Everyone got

"hilariously tight,'" one Guest Editor recalled, her "everyone" surely including fellow GE Miss Joan Didion.

Guest Editor Didion of Sacramento, California, arrived "with a drawer full of prizes and awards." A rising senior at the UC Berkeley campus, she flew for the first time in her life to a New York City that felt overwhelming and alien until she returned, a few years later, to live and work in Manhattan. By

1958, a job at *Vogue* lured her to the city, where she honed her prose by writing copy with tight word limits (e.g., "all through the house, color, verve, improvised treasures in happy but anomalous coexistence"). Didion (b. 1934) would launch her stellar literary career with the 1970 novel *Play It as It Lays* and go on to publish some fifteen books and numerous articles on literature and politics.

As a Guest Editor, Didion knew of Sylvia Plath (b. 1932), a Barbizon predecessor who had grown up in the Boston suburbs, attended Smith College in western Massachusetts, and was later to be widely acclaimed for darkly psychological poetry in the collections *Colossus* (1960) and the posthumous *Ariel* (1965). Plath's stint as a 1953 Guest Editor proved alternately tedious and bizarre, but she showcased the drinks tabulated by others in her exposé that saw print as the semi-autobiographical novel *The Bell Jar* (1963).

"I was supposed to be having the time of my life," opines the surrogate Sylvia, renamed the fictional Esther Greenwood (just as the Barbizon became the Amazon in Plath's novel, and a thinly disguised *Mademoiselle* was dubbed *Ladies' Day*). *The Bell Jar*'s antic episodes, corroborated by historian Bren, include a spoiled luncheon salad that fells the entire GE cadre with ptomaine, together with a bachelor apartment afternoon seduction with an Old Fashioned and vodka, and a blind date at a country club, where Sylvia/Esther downs numerous Daiquiris, just as she was photographed drinking Martinis "on some Starlight Roof," to all appearances "having a real whirl."

Readers realize early on that, tipsy or cold sober, a depressed Esther foresees a future of suffocating domestic servitude, though her anger-turned-inward is mistaken for lassitude. In the 1920s, the Barbizon's Molly Brown had proclaimed to a reporter, "The American girl can't hold her liquor; she shows it right away and grows mushy or wants to fight." The midcentury American girl, whether fueled by liquor or chamomile tea, too often mixed fury with a "mushy" submission to her fate as a wife and mother, her career plans forsaken. Journalist Betty Friedan diagnosed this "problem that has no name" to be midcentury America's "feminine mystique," and the Barbizonians of these years qualify as a "dollhouse" case study. The Guest Editors of 1953 "all wrote that they aspired to become wives, mothers (preferably of three children), while keeping up a career. But privately they said otherwise." Historian Bren pinpoints them as "the tightrope generation," quoting a poignant Guest Editor of 1953: "We were the first generation after the war and the last generation before the Pill."

"Fame and Fortune," nonetheless, awaited a remarkable number of midcentury Barbizonians. "Dana from Michigan," a dancer, was eyed in the hotel coffee shop by composer Gian Carlo Menotti and won a spot in the upcoming Spoleto Festival in Italy, while Betty Buckley wandered into an audition for the Broadway musical *1776*, won a role, and was later dubbed "the Voice of Broadway." Lorna Luft, a high school dropout at age seventeen and resident of the Barbizon (at her mother Judy Garland's insistence), appeared on Broadway in the musical *Lolita*, and Guest Editor–turned–film star Grace Kelly became Her Royal Highness when she married Prince Rainier of Monaco in April 1956. The first African American Guest Editor, Barbara Chase, was kept under wraps during the "extravagant fashion show" when the "GEs paraded down the runway," lest *Mademoiselle* and its advertisers lose the

Southern market. Barbara, however, soon enjoyed a paid internship at *Charm* magazine and a fellowship at the American Academy in Rome. Under her married name, Barbara Chase-Riboud, she became a "renowned visual artist, bestselling novelist, and award-winning poet."

The Barbizon began to falter with the feminist movement's challenge to sex discrimination, together with a recession that crippled the city's economy and the withdrawal of Katy Gibbs students in 1972. The building was renamed Barbizon 63A following a major renovation for condominium use and, in 1982, was placed on the National Register of Historic Places, out of time but never out of mind.

MANHATTAN

Ingredients:
1. 1½ ounces Canadian whisky
2. ¼ ounce sweet (Italian) vermouth
3. 2 dashes Angostura bitters
4. Maraschino cherry

Directions:
1. Fill mixing glass with ice cubes.
2. Add whisky and vermouth.
3. Add bitters.
4. Stir and strain into chilled cocktail glass.
5. Garnish with cherry and serve.

MARTINI

Ingredients:
1. 1½ ounces gin
2. ¼ ounce dry vermouth
3. Green olive (pitless)

Directions:
1. Fill mixing glass with ice cubes.
2. Add gin and vermouth.
3. Strain into chilled Martini glass.
4. Add olive and serve.

SCOTCH AND SODA
Ingredients:
1. 1–2 ounces scotch whisky
2. 4 ounces soda water
3. 3–4 ice cubes

Directions:
1. Put ice in whisky glass or Old Fashioned glass.
2. Add whisky.
3. Add soda water, stir gently, and serve.

OLD FASHIONED
Ingredients:
1. 2 ounces bourbon whiskey
2. 2 dashes Angostura bitters
3. 1 sugar cube
4. Soda water (uncarbonated if preferred)
5. Orange and lemon wedges
6. Maraschino cherry

Directions:
1. Put sugar cube in Old Fashioned glass.
2. Soak with bitters.
3. Add orange and lemon wedges and macerate.
4. Add ice and bourbon.
5. Fill with soda or water and stir gently.
6. Garnish with cherry and serve.

DAIQUIRI

Ingredients:
1. 2 ounces white rum
2. ¼–½ ounce sugar syrup
3. ¾ ounce fresh lime juice

Directions:
1. Put ample ice cubes in shaker.
2. Add rum, syrup, and lime juice.
3. Strain into chilled cocktail glass and serve.

3

GRAY FLANNEL SUITS

Tom put on his best suit, a freshly cleaned and pressed
gray flannel. On his way to work he stopped in Grand
Central Station to buy a clean white handkerchief and
have his shoes shined.

—Sloan Wilson, *The Man in the Gray Flannel Suit*, 1955

Young executives of the postwar fifties happily shed wartime
khakis and combat boots, but new uniforms fitted them for
upcoming battles for the executive suite. On-the-rise executives dared not step into rock 'n' roll's celebrated "Blue Suede
Shoes," nor opt for pinstripes or shadow plaids. Their suitcoats
and trousers of softly woven gray wool flannel announced
ambition and team spirit, as did their wingtips. The campaign
for the high-rise corner office with a menagerie of minions
on lower floors would require gray flannel at the desk, at the
meeting—and at the three-Martini lunch.

Sloan Wilson struck a chord with his fictional exposé of a
WWII veteran's tangled life, and the film version of *The Man
in the Gray Flannel Suit* (starring Gregory Peck) underscored
the tumult of the midcentury man whose battlefield experience collides with postwar ambition, family needs, and a com-
munity that means more than commuter rail convenience. A
Harvard graduate and US Coast Guard veteran who worked
as a reporter for *Time* and *Life* magazines, Wilson (b. 1920)
situated his flannel-suited, fictional Tom Rath somewhere

between a sociology database and a psychoanalyst's couch. As one flannel suit among many, Tom navigates the labyrinth of a gigantic media conglomerate while rivals undercut him in guerrilla skirmishes. The daily afterwork suburban "pitcher of martinis" mixed by his wife, Betsy, soothes his fevered brow, and the "half tumblerful of martinis" he takes upstairs at bedtime braces him for the next day, so he hopes.

Bestselling midcentury tomes presented the gray flannel labyrinth of big business as a spreadsheet open to public view. William H. Whyte's *The Organization Man* and C. Wright Mills's *White Collar* surveyed the corporate roster, from executives atop the hierarchy who are "calm and sober and unhurried" to the rigid "old veterans" desperate for "deference." (The CEO was to "be calm, judicious, rational" and to "groom" his personality.) Neither scholarly opus demeaned itself with advice on the junior executive's cocktail conduct nor offered wardrobe advice.

Not so *The Man in the Gray Flannel Suit*, which included a tutorial for the all-important job interview that, if successful, could send the candidate to midcentury's Valhalla as "a ten thousand dollar a year man." Once inside the executive suite, the job candidate must not be lulled by the corporate mogul's cordial demeanor ("So nice of you to come. . . . What can I get you to drink?"). Best to ignore the "forest of bottles," for the candidate's cue is the CEO's "I think I'll have Scotch on the rocks. Will that suit you?" The one and only answer: "That will be fine." (Time enough for other libations when the candidate is on the payroll and sipping "bourbon on the rocks" with the boss and traveling on an expense account, enjoying his Martini at a hotel where "a lighted pyramid of bottles revolved slowly" on "an ornate circular bar.")

Midcentury corporate behemoths ranged from entertainment to manufacturing, such as the furniture maker in *Executive Suite*, the novel where bourbon and Martinis punctuate the rivals' days, but cocktails signal an illicit affair in a single woman's out-of-town apartment. ("Will it spoil your cocktail," she coyly asks, "if you sit here in the kitchen and watch me start dinner?" Chances are, she stowed a bottle of

Seagram's in a kitchen cabinet.) Beyond manufacturing, the movies, and explosive network television, other gray flannel careers sprang up on Madison Avenue, where advertising took its place with "such long-standing institutions as the school and the church in the magnitude of its social influence." The new "Madman," according to historian David Potter, "dominates the media" and exerts "vast power in the shaping of popular standards." Advertising megastar Mary Wells Lawrence well knew how powerfully advertising impacted culture at home and abroad, though the social side of business perplexed this executive who disliked drinking but "decided that martinis looked sophisticated, especially if you were holding a cigarette." (Wells Lawrence "concentrated on martinis" until she found them palatable.)

The gray flannel generation found itself at a crossroads between earnest devotion to corporate America and the iconoclastic humor that bubbled like a satire by Mark Twain. Fusing Detroit's automobiles to the Stars and Stripes by 1953, General Motors' chief, Charles E. Wilson (nicknamed "Engine Charlie"), was widely quoted and somewhat misquoted, but the gist was clear: "What is good for General Motors is good for the country, and what is good for the country is good for General Motors." GM, like kindred corporate behemoths, was thought to be an impersonal, highly efficient business operating like a well-oiled machine.

Humor played its midcentury part when a big-business spoof reached print and became a wildly popular Broadway musical. Shepherd Mead's *How to Succeed in Business without Really Trying* tapped a satirical vein of American humor in an easy-access how-to guide to the executive suite. The company must be "BIG" in a "BIG CITY," and the job seeker "an all-around man of no special ability." The chapters spooled from "How to Rise from the Mail Room" to "How to Play Company Politics" to "How to Stop Being a Junior Executive" ("Be Decisive," but "Avoid a Decision"). In memos, "Never Come Straight to the Point." Be a "Ray of Sunshine," but memorize useful phrases, e.g., "You may not see it in the figures, but the trend is obvious."

As for the up-and-coming exec's dress, *How to Succeed in Business without Really Trying* advised that "the local pawnshop will supply you with school rings, ties, pins, pennants, and old footballs painted with historic scores." Otherwise, the young man must scale the corporate heights in gray flannel suits from the august men's clothier Brooks Brothers. Founded in New York City in 1818, Brooks Brothers promised "to make and deal only in merchandise of the finest body . . . and to deal with people who seek and appreciate such merchandise." US presidents from Abraham Lincoln to John F. Kennedy favored Brooks Brothers suits, as did diplomats and captains of industry. The company introduced a line of Harris tweed and Shetland sweaters, but the man on the midcentury corporate ladder must choose the clothier's one-and-only gray flannel suit, according to *How to Succeed in Business without Really Trying*. A cartoon diagrammed the young businessman at the start of his day, complete with briefcase and an overcoat folded over one arm. From his haircut to his eyeglasses, from his aftershave to his shoes and socks, one brand name only: Brooks Brothers.

Sloan Wilson's title became a humorous catchphrase, his earnest effort to protest against the hidebound postwar suburban life twisted into "a sort of national joke in the United States." Tailors offered to measure the author for free flannel suits, and *Mad* magazine published a takedown of the novel. A skit on TV's popular sitcom *The Honeymooners* featured plumber Ed Norton (played by Art Carney) emerging from the sewer to crack to pal Ralph Kramden (Jackie Gleason), "What did you expect, the man in the gray flannel suit?" Recalled author Wilson, ruefully, "People often roared in high hilarity when they said to me, 'Are you the guy who wrote *The Man in the Gray Flannel Suit?*'" He did not reveal his answer when the laughter died down.

THE GIN MARTINI
Ingredients:
1. 2 ounces gin
2. ½ teaspoon dry vermouth
3. Small pitless green olive

Directions:
1. Fill mixing glass with ample ice and chill.
2. Add gin and vermouth.
3. Stir (but avoid meltage).
4. Strain into cold Martini glass.
5. Garnish with olive and serve.

SCOTCH ON THE ROCKS
Ingredients:
1. 1–2 ounces scotch whisky
2. 3–4 clear, hard, coldest ice cubes

Directions:
1. Put ice in Old Fashioned glass.
2. Pour whisky over the ice.
3. Stir very briefly and serve.

BOURBON ON THE ROCKS

Ingredients:
1. 1–2 ounces bourbon whiskey
2. 3–4 clear, hard, coldest ice cubes

Directions:
1. Put ice in Old Fashioned glass.
2. Pour whiskey over the ice.
3. Stir very briefly and serve.

SEAGRAM'S SEVEN CROWN COCKTAIL

Ingredients:
1. 1½ ounces Seagram's whiskey
2. ½ ounce lemon juice
3. 1 teaspoon sugar
4. 2 dashes Angostura bitters

Directions:
1. Put ample ice in shaker.
2. Add all ingredients and shake well.
3. Strain into chilled cocktail glass or serve over ice in Old Fashioned glass.

4

THE BAR CAR

Cocktails on the rails refreshed thirsty commuters and travelers, but the Broadway Limited and the California Zephyr were distant cousins of the "5:29" or the "6:02," as commuters called their trains. Alluring names like the Zephyr, the Admiral, or the Acadian meant cocktails or highballs crafted to order and sipped at leisure by travelers who socialized or enjoyed the passing scenery. Not so for commuters on the New Haven "5:29" or Long Island Railroad "6:02" who slaked thirst on rails to the suburbs. For them, the bar car was the limbo between the city's workday strife and the three-ring circus waiting at home. The first bar car drink promised respite from the tedious meeting and the boss's ominous warning, and the second or third round fortified commuters soon to learn that the washing machine flooded at home or the children had come down with chicken pox.

A "decorous rolling saloon" quipped social critic A. C. Spectorsky of the bar car scene; his tally found that "the most crowded trains are those that leave between five-thirty and six" to bring "whisky-drinking males" to their home dinner tables. The bar car, he added, "is always filled to overflowing," mostly with men but also counting "the hard-bitten female copy writer clutching a dollar bill at the ready." The car's two bartenders coped with crates and cases of "Canadian Club and Old Grand Dad, of Ballantine and White Rock and Canada Dry . . . of Schweppes and Heublein

martinis." By 6 p.m., "forty people in the car, their cries for booze filled the air." By the time the train pulled out, "all the glasses were gone, and drinks were being served in paper cups."

The bar car featured in midcentury fiction when novelist Max Shulman put his suburban commuter, Harry Bannerman, on the club car of the New Haven Railroad's "5:29" in *Rally Round the Flag, Boys!*, a bestseller that spoofed the postwar suburban scene in a borderline farce underpinned with edgy critique. True to his tribe, Harry wears gray flannel suits and diligently toils at his desk in the city, but his suburban Connecticut home in the quaint village of Putnam's Landing "cost more money than Harry was making," and his typical day's "timetable" had become a slurry of hours come and gone.

The bartender who serves Harry his second bar car bourbon credits the past president of the New Haven Railroad for saving more marriages than "the church, the state, and the psychiatrists all put together." True, "the trains were late, the cars were filthy, and the service was miserable," but the man had the genius to "put club cars in the commuter trains."

Harry understood. As the train approached the Putnam's Landing station, he "tossed off his bourbon, and, less anesthetized than he would have liked, walked slowly to the door." If sobriety were the rule, the novel insists, America's bar car husbands could not face the home front.

BOURBON AND WATER
Ingredients:
1. 1½ ounces bourbon whiskey
2. 2–3 ounces mineral water
3. 3–4 hard, clear ice cubes
Directions:
1. Put ice in Old Fashioned glass.
2. Add whiskey.
3. Add water as desired and serve.

HEUBLEIN MARTINI ON THE ROCKS
Ingredients:
1. 1½ ounces Heublein Martini (brand containing London dry gin and dry vermouth)
2. 3–4 hard, clear ice cubes
Directions:
1. Put ice into Old Fashioned glass.
2. Add Heublein Martini, stir, and serve.

NEW HAVEN BAR CAR DOUBLE SCOTCH
(weekday trains between 5:00 and 7:00 p.m.)
> *Ingredients:*
>   1. 3 ounces Ballantine scotch whisky
>   2. 3–4 ice cubes
> *Directions:*
>   1. Put ice in slug-bottom glass.
>   2. Pour in whisky and serve.

5

LE WEEKEND

Trains, a few planes, countless automobiles—and the weekend gets underway on Friday evening! High-flying salesmen will exit aircraft and taxi home, while suburban train platforms bustle with men in gray flannel suits and colorfully dressed wives and children who hasten to the parking lot for the family station wagon and a short drive home. Other commuting breadwinners, meanwhile, have taken the wheel to head home from the city, pulled off the highways to the subdivision and, finally, into the driveway of home sweet home. The front door opened, and the children rushed to cry, "Daddy!" The weekend had begun.

The jampacked prelude to Friday-to-Sunday revels rested with the homemaker, who was spared obligations for midweek shindigs but double-checked her weekend lists over Friday morning's second cup of coffee. With her husband off to work and the children in school, her day now began. A lifetime ago, she might have worked in the city, but marriage and children took her to the suburbs as a full-time homemaker. Her workweek, capsuled in interviews by journalist Betty Friedan, consumed every minute of the day: shopping, chauffeuring, filling washers and dryers, ironing, cooking, waxing, polishing, vacuuming, gardening, helping with children's homework, collecting for charities. Perhaps her "dearest ambition is an absolutely well-ordered and efficiently run house," or else she feels it is "nonsense" to obsess over the household. Either way, quipped satirist Russell Lynes, "It boils down to a conflict between two aphorisms—'cleanliness is next to godliness' and 'a little dirt never hurt anybody.'" Whichever it might be, the lady of the house shouldered responsibility for *le weekend* preparations, stockpiling food and beverages from the supermarket and the local liquor store.

The "package stores" had long displayed distilled spirits in masculine trappings with pirates, cavaliers, and big game animals on labels and cartons. One midcentury advertising copywriter, Dorothy Diamond, scolded male colleagues for presuming whiskey and gin were consumed only by "clubmen, sportsman, and men in evening clothes." In the mid-1950s, *Vogue* magazine surveyed four hundred retail stores and found 38 percent of the dealers reporting that one-half of their customers were women. "The women evidently were ignoring many of the old taboos about liquor," concluded Vance Packard's *The Hidden Persuaders*, "because liquor stores were starting to be grouped in shopping centers." The popular sociologist's opus on advertising underscored Dorothy Diamond's advice that "the liquor people could do a much better job . . . with festive windows and well-styled interiors." Catering to men only, the average liquor store was "as listless as a leftover highball."

Distillers took their cue. Labels changed, and some high-shoulder whiskey bottles morphed into sleek decanters, while the United States Brewers' Association urged "female-oriented ads, nice packaging, and display" because women bought beer "from their weekly food budgets." (Budweiser introduced a slim new can, bowing to "the innate preference of women for grace, beauty, and style," while Pabst's new slogan decreed, "The finest is always in fashion.") Vintners, for their part, faced customers' fears of committing *faux pas* by choosing the "wrong" wine, the "wrong" year, and the "wrong" glass.

Advertisers urged "the wine folks" to cease the esoteric "nonsense" and to "hammer" the message that "any wine is good no matter how you serve it." Wine merchants followed suit "with considerable success."

The weekend commenced at home Friday evening with the premise that "one martini will do wonders." With her husband momentarily busy with the children, the lady of the house "dropped five ice cubes into her glass martini pitcher, added three ounces of gin and a half ounce of Noilly Prat, stirred," and poured the first of numerous libations to ferry the couple through the weekend. Perhaps the man of the house secretly thought himself deserving a medal for his hard week in the city, so the homemaker had best bank his hunger with chips or cheese-and-crackers until dinner was on the table. Tonight, the sitter was coming, and the couple would join friends for an evening at the theater, where they are season ticket holders, followed by nightcaps at a café that stayed open very late, perhaps discussing the play they saw over a Negroni or an Irish Fix, if not a Vodka Grand Marnier or a New York Sour.

Saturday's daylight hours often belonged to Dad and the children, for "Dad is suddenly, wonderfully at home all the time." Perhaps he "spoils them, takes them to the toy store . . . and spends five times their allowance buying them gifts more suitable to Christmas or birthdays, and plays with them endlessly." The children's own schedules often took command at midcentury as they do at the present day. Little League baseball, peewee football, small-fry tennis lessons, and instructions in ice skating, hockey, field sports, swimming, softball . . . the list goes on. Perhaps Dad coaches a team, so hours are hived off for his weekly stint at the ballfield, the playground, or the gym. Or Dad manages a round of golf, at least nine holes, preferably eighteen

with highballs afterward in the clubhouse or on the terrace. By five o'clock, with the first Gin and Tonics in hand, the dartboard might beckon for the final athletic contest of the day.

Saturday night, however, belonged to the couples. The sitter returned, the children were fed, and the twosome dressed for the evening: a coat and tie for him, and for her, a cocktail dress, high heels, jewelry, and cosmetics by Helena Rubinstein (and her favorite perfume, perhaps Joy by Jean Patou or Chanel No. 5 in the new spray cologne bottle). The couple prepped with Martinis, and they set out by 7 p.m., alerting the sitter to expect them back well after midnight. Social critic A.

C. Spectorsky observed that affluent, exurban couples especially dreaded "being left out on Saturday night," and thus the night's enticements "beckon too urgently."

Restaurant dinners foregrounded a round of parties, large and small, for "parties are their night life," and Saturday night's partying kept all in the social swim. Perhaps dinner at a charming "Early American" inn might begin at seven over a specialty drink such as the Manhasset cocktail. Alternately, a steakhouse might beckon, prompting predinner chitchat over preferred cocktails, while red wines would be matched with the thickest beefsteaks to be grilled rare, medium, or well-done (the T-bone to be bagged for the family dog). Ashtrays appeared on the white tablecloth, and cigarettes were alight throughout the meal at every table. "Hopes are high that one will really have fun, this time. . . . The pre-party fantasies are riotous, the search for relaxation from tension more imperious, the chatter higher pitched, and the smiles more brilliant."

A major topic of conversation at the parties: real estate, "stories of sales and resales, of acreage and property, of zoning and building and remodeling." The men's careers nudged inevitably into conversations, who has been favored by a recent promotion, or who else took a prized job out from under so-and-so's nose at the agency or the firm. "Everybody knows everybody else, and they are all on at least their second drinks." Before three dozen guests depart, "they will have put a severe dent in their host's liquor supply . . . a half case of Scotch, a half case of gin, a half case of rye, and a half case of bourbon will see him through the evening." The partygoers lounge, at last, on couches with drinks in hand, reluctant to call it a night. The wee hours are upon them, and they will be at home and asleep "by three-thirty."

Sunday, a day of relaxation, will begin with churchgoing and Sunday school for the children, for "the postwar revival of interest in organized religion, noticeable all over the country," has brought weekenders to the church of their choice. The Sunday newspapers might take an hour, but at noon, according to one account, "You can hear someone say, 'I don't know about you, but I think I'll have a martini.'" Brunch leads into a long afternoon fending off the children's pleas for amusement. ("Daddy is not a toy. . . . Go find something to play with.") No formal parties have been planned, but by late Sunday afternoon, friends call friends without notice: "You doing anything? Come on over. . . . You stuck at home with the kids? We'll be over. You need any gin?" The "housecrawling" begins as the sun sinks and the moon rises. Jokes about tomorrow's "rat race" sneak into conversation, and by bedtime, the alarm clocks are set. *Le weekend* has come . . . and gone.

NOILLY PRAT MARTINI (FOR TWO)

Ingredients:
1. 3 ounces gin
2. ½ ounce Noilly Prat dry vermouth

Directions:
1. Put 4 or 5 ice cubes in Martini pitcher.
2. Add Noilly Prat.
3. Stir, pour, and serve in Martini glasses.

MANHASSET COCKTAIL

Ingredients:
1. 1½ ounces blended whiskey
2. ¼ ounce sweet vermouth
3. ¼ ounce dry vermouth
4. Lemon peel

Directions:
1. Fill shaker with ice.
2. Vigorously shake whiskey and both sweet and dry vermouth.
3. Strain into prechilled cocktail glass.
4. Squeeze lemon peel over the top, drop it into the glass, and serve.

NEGRONI

Ingredients:
1. ¾ ounce gin
2. ¾ ounce Campari
3. ¾ ounce sweet vermouth

Directions:
1. Fill mixing glass with ice.
2. Add ingredients and stir well.

3. Strain into prechilled cocktail glass. (May be served on the rocks with a splash of soda and/or lemon twist.)

IRISH FIX

Ingredients:
1. 2 ounces Irish whiskey
2. 1 teaspoon sugar
3. 2 teaspoons water
4. ½ ounce lemon juice
5. 2 teaspoons Irish Mist
6. ½ slice orange
7. ½ slice lemon

Directions:
1. In 8-ounce glass, dissolve sugar in water.
2. Add whiskey and lemon juice.
3. Fill glass with crushed ice.
4. Stir well and add ice to the top.
5. Garnish with orange and lemon slices.
6. Float Irish Mist on top and serve.

VODKA GRAND MARNIER

Ingredients:
1. 1½ ounces vodka
2. ½ ounce Grand Marnier
3. ½ ounce lime juice
4. 1 slice orange

Directions:
1. Fill shaker with ice.
2. Add vodka, Grand Marnier, and lime juice.
3. Shake vigorously.
4. Strain over rocks into prechilled Old Fashioned glass.
5. Garnish with orange slice.

NEW YORK SOUR

Ingredients:
1. 2 ounces blended whiskey
2. Chilled dry red wine
3. ½ ounce lemon juice
4. 1 teaspoon sugar
5. ½ slice lemon

Directions:
1. Put ample ice in shaker.
2. Vigorously shake whiskey, lemon juice, and sugar.
3. Strain into 6-ounce sour glass.
4. Fill glass with red wine.
5. Stir, garnish with lemon slice, and serve.

WHISKEY HIGHBALL

Ingredients:
1. 2 ounces whiskey
2. 4–6 ounces club soda or ginger ale

Directions:
1. Fill highball glass with ice.
2. Add whiskey.
3. Slowly add soda water or ginger ale.
4. Stir gently and serve.

GIN AND TONIC

Ingredients:
1. 2 ounces gin
2. 6 ounces tonic water
3. Wedge or slice of lime

Directions:
1. Fill highball glass with ice cubes.
2. Add gin.
3. Slowly add tonic water.
4. Stir gently, add lime, and serve.

6

PULITZERS VERSUS POTBOILERS

A "battle of the books" roiled when literary Olympians laced up the gloves to face off against mass market authors in a contest pitting prestige against sales and cold, hard cash. Midcentury rivalries went rounds in the marketplace, and books became the arena where sales figures punched against artistic merit, while stocks rose and fell as critics weighed in and bank statements signaled a knockout. Whether promoting a blockbuster bestseller or a literary showpiece, however, both sides claimed neutrality where alcohol was concerned. The pleasures and pains of booze suffused pages authored by the elite and the popular in the midcentury battle of the books. Both found common cause in authors' reliance on drinks, which flowed freely through potboilers and prizewinners without prejudice to either side. Drinks, in short, became authors' equal opportunity asset.

Best known for honoring excellence in journalism, the Pulitzer Prize also lent its sheen to poets, novelists, and short story writers. A Hungarian Jewish immigrant who studied law, Joseph Pulitzer (b. 1847) became a US citizen and successful newspaper publisher in St. Louis before the New York *World* brought him a fortune. His last will and testament established Pulitzer Prizes to promote excellence in journalism and, among other categories, to honor achievement in "letters and drama." Like the Good Housekeeping Seal of Approval, the coveted imprimatur of a Pulitzer Prize certified quality and hyped book sales, though winners were loath to admit the monetary heft of a medal underpinned by a modest check.

Novelists' newest titles caught attention, but short stories also competed in midcentury years when readers opened the weekly highbrow *New Yorker* magazine to find fiction by Jean Stafford (b. 1915) or John O'Hara (b. 1905), if not John Cheever (b. 1912). All three mirrored modern social drinking, from O'Hara's "very light scotch on the rocks" ("The Weakling") to Stafford's noontime "Bloody Marys" ("Cops and Robbers"), though Cheever's stories more deeply probed the dark side of boozing, as in "The Sorrows of Gin" in which the juniper berry distillate is implicated in the demise of a hard-drinking woman who dies in Bellevue, known as "America's most storied hospital." Cheever's Pulitzer for his collected short stories arrived in 1979, but, in grisly irony, O'Hara died the year Jean Stafford won the 1970 Pulitzer that had eluded her fellow scribe. (All three writers "double-dipped" when their stories appeared in published collections, but all three launched careers with *de rigueur* full-length novels, O'Hara's *Appointment in Samarra*, Stafford's *Boston Adventure*, and Cheever's *The Wapshot Chronicle*.)

Heated book reviews, all the while, debated the elusive literary quality of the stories and novels as reviewers hailed the bookstore worthies and dismissed drugstore wire-rack pulps. Complicit in the struggle, readers knew their book choices measured personal taste, the adjutant of quality. Gender played its part in the devil's dance of prestige against profit, especially when women authors sold bestselling "potboilers" to Hollywood for the lucrative silver screen. No matter how these frictions resolved (or did not), writers and readers could be certain that midcentury titles featured cocktails, highballs,

and liquor served neat or on the rocks. Sipped or swigged, midcentury libations were authors' stock-in-trade.

The rancorous debate over merit and money—and gender—was longstanding in US literary history, for women novelists of the preceding century had outsold male compatriots in a genre both loved and derided as sentimental. The widely read E.D.E.N. Southworth (Emma Dorothy Eliza Nevitte Southworth, b. 1819) penned some sixty novels, and sales of Harriet Beecher Stowe's *Uncle Tom's Cabin* came second only to the Bible's. Nathaniel Hawthorne's notorious 1855 critique of a "damned mob of scribbling women" rang true for him when sales of *The Scarlet Letter* petered out after a promising launch, despite Hawthorne's choice of a surefire stock character featured in scores of sentimental bestsellers. Hawthorne's fallen woman, Hester Prynne, did not spark robust sales.

Fast forward to the 1950s, and the bad boy writer and self-styled public intellectual Norman Mailer (b. 1923) dismissed contemporary women writers as lightweights. ("I can only say that the sniffs I get from the ink of the women are always fey, old hat, Quaintsy . . . stillborn.") He grudgingly admitted the "early" work of Carson McCullers, Jean Stafford, and Mary McCarthy gave him "pleasure," but McCarthy's bestselling 1963 novel *The Group* fired him up once again. McCarthy's story of eight fictional Vassar College graduates who wend their troublesome ways through the 1930s Depression years struck Mailer as a "flatly written . . . fiasco," a "trivial lady writer's novel." A WWII veteran (and eventual two-time Pulitzer winner), Mailer had first won fame with *The Naked and the Dead*, a 1948 war novel accented with beer and army camp hooch. He proceeded to pen a fictional critique of Hollywood nabobs in *The Deer Park* (1955), in which a thinly disguised Palm Springs boasts a popular bar named the Hangover.

As book reviewer, Mailer overlooked Mary McCarthy's reliance on the libations he himself had tapped for fiction: case in point, *The Group*'s young women's "fascination" with the Brandy Alexander, Clover Club, and White Lady cocktails they "adored." Mailer also ignored McCarthy's cue to readers about the newlyweds who imbibe "cocktails every night in the aluminum cocktail shaker," with the bride's love of "formality" against her hubby's zest for "the liquor." The philandering husband's cocktail party savvy with "a tray of drinks" augurs his descent into "straight liquor" and the marital crack-up, while the bride who has sipped cocktails poured from an art deco Russel Wright shaker ends her life in a tumble from the high-rise Vassar Club.

The cocktail party was itself endowed with serious timely themes when the renowned poet, essayist, and playwright T. S. Eliot, author of *The Waste Land*, framed his exploration of marriage, infidelity, and the shallows of adult life in his

1949 stage drama *The Cocktail Party*. A character scripted as "Unidentified Guest" is revealed as a marriage counseling psychiatrist (first played by Alec Guinness), and he requests gin with water ("sip it slowly . . . and drink it sitting down"). Ultimately, he stitches the hosts' fractured marriage together, but not until the audience withstands three theatrical acts of characters so drunk on their dialogue that the reason for the gathering feels inconsequential.

The cocktail party stakes rose higher, the gin more vivid in Jean Stafford's 1948 *New Yorker* short story "Children Are Bored on Sunday," which vivisects the New York cocktail party scene from the outlook of Emma, a shy young home-town "rube" who frequents the Metropolitan Museum on Sunday afternoons for the love of Botticelli but feels attracted to a slender young man she eyes in the galleries, drawn to his "El Greco face." He hasn't yet seen her, but she has been a guest at his recent cocktail parties on Madison Avenue, parties that left her feeling "shaky with apprehensions and martinis, and with the belligerence of a child who feels . . . laughed at."

His cocktail parties become entrée to Stafford's literary pa-thology lab, her scalpel the young woman's nervous naivete in the face of bewildering pseudo-sophistication. Filled with "cun-ning guests, on their guard and highly civilized," the pretentious parties proceed in a new "stylized" etiquette, "unlike any par-ties" Emma "had known at home." Puzzling allusions and ref-erences sound like private codewords ("Hindemith," "Sartre," "Franco," "Henry Luce," "the Atomic Energy Commission"). The plentiful gin Martinis, however, incite arguments that end "in a bloody nose and black eye." Emma had seen this slugfest repeatedly but "could not believe that city people clipped each other's jaws," that the urbane cocktail party was, at base, "an occasion for getting drunk." Better the taverns back home, she feels, with "delicious amber whisky in a joint with a jukebox, a stout barkeep, and a handful of tottering derelicts." Stafford offers an apparently happy ending when "El Greco" spots Emma leaving the museum and approaches her. "Can I buy you a drink, Emma?" As if a heart were carved on an apple tree: "Intellectual Loves Rube." The "children" can play on Sunday afternoon, now that Stafford's dissection has come to its close.

The cocktail party rose like a phoenix when playwright Edward Albee saw New York ripening for a stage play based on recent fictional exposés of the collegiate ivory tower as a nest of rivalries, petty politics, and grievances. What better high drama in 1962 than a cocktail party set in the groves of academe, assisted by brandy, bourbon, gin, and superb performances by Uta Hagen and Arthur Hill at Broadway's Billy Rose Theatre? Audiences flocked to *Who's Afraid of Virginia Woolf?*, in which a midlife married couple, George and Martha, rage to their marrow over soul-crushing disappointments from infertility to his stalled academic career, all the while ensnaring a guileless young couple invited to their home for a "nightcap."

Who's Afraid of Virginia Woolf? took theatergoers into a rough-and-tumble *Walpurgisnacht*, just as rapt moviegoers' pulses quickened at Elizabeth Taylor and Richard Burton as George and Martha on the big screen when Mike Nichols directed filmdom's reprise in 1966. Audiences might have wished to sip Martha's favorite cocktails of years past, for George remembers her Brandy Alexanders, gimlets, and frappés, all the while gin and booze on the rocks punctuate the three-hour drama. (As for the Pulitzer Prize in drama, Albee's play was initially declared the winner, but the original decision was overridden because the play did not portray a "wholesome" view of American life, and its sexual themes and language were not deemed "uplifting.")

Pulitzer Prize selection juries disdained potboilers, defined by *Webster's* in 1960 as works of "art or literature, often inferior, produced only to make money." Authors Grace Metalious (b. 1924) and Jacqueline Susann (b. 1918) could have "laughed all the way to the bank," as the adage goes, for Metalious's *Peyton Place* (1956) and Susann's *The Valley of the Dolls* (1966) surged as blockbuster fiction with intricate, hair-raising, sexy plots that sold tens of millions of copies and segued from print to the silver screen. Metalious and Susann bookended the midcentury years with fervid, melodramatic storylines, from Metalious's picture-postcard New England small town riven with abuse, betrayals, and violated taboos to Susann's Broadway backstage and Hollywood sets replete with cheated lovers, thwarted amour, and stars' careers on the skids. Susann's "dolls" referenced the new tranquilizing pills marketed to "take the edge off" anxiety, but alcohol flows in her novel as it does in *Peyton Place*, calming nerves, speeding up seduction, and drowning guilt and sorrows.

Mercenary motives aside, both authors wrote in good faith to the best of their abilities. Metalious bet readers would find *Peyton Place* captivating from its opening: "Indian summer is like a woman, hotly passionate, but fickle, she comes and goes as she pleases so that one is never sure whether she will come at all, nor whether she will stay. . . . One year, early in October, Indian summer came to a town called Peyton Place."

Jacqueline Susann, for her part, wagered with equal fervor that her opus would be the page-turner she expected it to be: "You've got to climb to the top of Mount Everest to reach the Valley of the Dolls. It's a brutal climb to reach that peak, which so few have seen."

Awash in monumental sales as *Peyton Place* and *The Valley of the Dolls* broke records, both infuriated authors saw their novels become grist for highbrow critics who sneered at "a small town peep show" (*Peyton Place*) and at the tabloid reader "who has put away comic books but isn't yet ready for editorials in *The Daily News*" (*The Valley of the Dolls*). Neither author enjoyed a long life, Grace Metalious passing at age thirty-nine, Susann at fifty-six, but both had the last laugh in sales. *Peyton Place* scored about eight and one-half million copies, and *The Valley of the Dolls* has passed thirty million copies. The drinks in their pages are many, each author her own midcentury toastmistress.

MARTINI (12 TO 1)

Ingredients
1. 2 ounces gin
2. 1 teaspoon dry vermouth
3. Pitless olive

Directions:
1. Add ice cubes to mixing glass.
2. Add gin and vermouth and stir until fully chilled.
3. Strain into cocktail glass, add olive, and serve.

WHITE LADY COCKTAIL

Ingredients:
1. 2 ounces gin
2. ½ ounce triple sec
3. ½ ounce fresh lemon juice
4. 1 egg white

Directions:
1. Add all ingredients to empty shaker and shake vigorously.
2. Add ice and shake again until well chilled.
3. Strain into cocktail glass and serve.

CLOVER CLUB COCKTAIL

Ingredients:
1. 1½ ounces gin
2. 1 teaspoon grenadine
3. ½ egg white

Directions:
1. Add ample ice to shaker.
2. Add all ingredients.
3. Shake vigorously, strain into cocktail glass, and serve.

BRANDY ALEXANDER COCKTAIL
Ingredients:
1. ¾ ounce brandy
2. ¾ ounce crème de cacao
3. ¾ ounce heavy cream

Directions:
1. Fill shaker with ice.
2. Add all ingredients.
3. Shake well, strain, and serve.

GIMLET
Ingredients:
1. 2 ounces gin
2. ½ ounce Rose's lime juice

Directions:
1. Put ample ice in mixing glass.
2. Add gin and lime juice and stir thoroughly.
3. Strain and serve in prechilled cocktail glass.

CELTIC FRAPPÉ
Ingredients:
1. 2 ounces Irish whiskey liqueur
2. ¾ ounce dry vermouth
3. ¼ ounce Pernod or absinthe
4. ¼ ounce orange ice
5. 1 dash Peychaud's bitters
6. Orange peel (for garnish)

Directions:
1. Fill shaker with ice.
2. Add all ingredients except orange peel.
3. Shake vigorously.

4. Strain into rocks glass filled with crushed ice.
5. Squeeze orange peel over glass to release flavor and drop into glass.

RYE AND GINGER HIGHBALL
Ingredients
1. 2 ounces rye whiskey
2. 4–6 ounces chilled ginger ale

Directions:
1. Put 5–6 ice cubes in highball glass.
2. Add whiskey.
3. Fill to top with ginger ale, stir gently, and serve.

7

BUNNIES AND PLAYBOYS

Step into the Spotlight . . . Be a Playboy Bunny . . .
An exciting new life awaits you if you're a pretty
young girl and you want to be a Bunny.
—Newspaper "wanted" advertisement, 1962

The want ads popped up in Chicago, New York, Miami, New Orleans, Dallas, Atlanta, and other cities in the US and abroad. The wild success of Hugh Hefner's *Playboy* magazine in the 1950s had whet appetites for a sophisticated gentlemen's club, and the Playboy brand promised a bonanza for clubs that opened nationwide in the following decade and beyond. Keyholding members by the tens of thousands arrived solo or brought friends or dates for drinks, dinner, and shows, but the entertainment mainstays were Bunnies, a hutch of smiling young women clad in satin rabbit ears and scanty thigh-high gleaming bodysuits with deepest cleavage and puffy rear-end white cottontails. French cuffs with Playboy logo cufflinks banded both wrists and, at the neck, a white shirt collar with black bow tie completed the ensemble, not to mention the dark stockings and stiletto heels. From the Bunny greeter at the club's front door to the Bunnies who checked coats, served drinks, or sold cigarettes, the young women branded the Playboy Club as the club branded them.

The Playboy mastermind, Hugh Hefner (b. 1926), had grown up in the Midwest as the son of a conservative schoolteacher and accountant father who raised Hugh and younger brother Keith in the Methodist church. Serving in WWII as a reporter for an Army newspaper, Hefner went on to a BA from the University of Illinois, majoring in creative writing and art. Graduate school in sociology at Northwestern University proved briefly attractive, as did his marriage, but Hefner dropped out to become a copywriter at *Esquire*. The preeminent US men's magazine since 1932, *Esquire* appeared on magazine racks alongside hunting and fishing monthlies and "girlie" magazines, and the canny Hefner foresaw the potential in a men's magazine he might launch by scraping together loans from family and friends. *Playboy* debuted in 1953 and catered, as Hefner wrote, to the new "male zeitgeist" of "an alert man, an aware man, a man of taste, a man sensitive to pleasure, a man who—without acquiring the stigma of a voluptuary or dilettante—can live life to the hilt." *Playboy* carried serious articles on culture and politics (Ray Bradbury's dystopian *Fahrenheit 451* appeared as a three-part serial), but the "hilt" was the "Playmate of the Month," a voluptuous *femme* who might be adorned solely in a diamond necklace and earrings, or, in December, a Santa Claus cap.

Successor to the popular magazine that paved the way for success, the Playboy Clubs demanded careful planning, and Hefner allied with a partner, Victor Lowndes III, a wealthy playboy, i.e., a rich bachelor gadabout. Both he and Hefner were divorced, and both bent to the task of club design that "presented an intoxicating mix of food and alcohol, music and entertainment in a sophisticated, sexually charged atmosphere." A lifetime membership would cost twenty-five dollars, entitling the Keyholder to the complimentary full buffet and access to all facilities in all the clubs.

A triumph from the start, the first Playboy Club opened in downtown Chicago at 116 E. Walton Street on the lucky leap year date of February 29, 1960. The backlighted entrance suggested a Mondrian abstract painting, and the teak and leather furnishings styled the club as distinctly midcentury modern. Recalled longtime bartender and manager John Dante, "the lobby was the center of the action. A member coming in from Walton Street . . . had to be impressed by the burst of sound and activity." From the lobby, he might make a reservation for the two showrooms, each presenting three shows nightly. Featured artists might include jazz pianist Bobby Short or vocalist Mabel Mercer, the Ramsey Lewis Trio or comedian Lenny Bruce. In addition to the showrooms and a Living Room, three other rooms enticed members: the softly candlelit Library where a date could be impressed after dinner; the ultra-sophisticated Penthouse; and the Playmate Bar with five working bartenders that became a waiting room for members without reservations. "When the Bar was filled to capacity, people would have to wait outside the club. . . . And it was common to have a waiting line outside that extended four abreast . . . sometimes in freezing temperatures."

This "Disneyland for Adults" drew Bunny hopefuls who fancied a change of pace from mundane routine and hungered for tips that meant good money. Tryouts lured young women from the college classroom and the Vegas chorus line, the secretarial desk and the bank teller window ("Please bring a swimsuit or leotards"). None knew that the Bunny idea initially "underwhelmed" Hefner and Lowndes, who thought the costume too much like a swimsuit, and besides, the Playboy rabbit logo was male. Cut high up the hip, however, and tweaked with fluffy ears and cottontail, "the Playboy Club

had a uniform for its servers." Add the collar, tie, and cuffs, and the Bunnies became iconic. One strict club rule provided a personal "bonus" of sorts: the big tips incurred no obligatory "dates." Bunnies were not "B" girls nor waitresses, much less hookers. A New York City license commissioner carped about "scantily clad waitresses," but young women flocked to audition, though the odds favored the house. For each hundred who applied for the "Spotlight," about twenty became Playboy Club Bunnies.

The rigorous route to showtime at the club, as Kathryn Leigh Scott reveals in her memoir, *The Bunny Years*, demanded "Boot Camp" training based on a system of merits and demerits. "Absenteeism, crooked ears, chewing gum or eating in front of customers" nicked trainees whose supervising Bunny Mother's "drill sergeant" deadpan tone struck the trainees as both funny and frightening. The Bunny Training Quiz must be passed, with such questions as:

IF A GUEST REMAINS SEATED FOR ONE HOUR AFTER HE HAS PAID THE CHECK:

a) Are you still responsible for his table?
b) Do you remove his empty glass?
c) Do you bring him 14 glasses of water if requested?
d) Do you keep checking to see if he'd like anything?
e) If he decides to have another drink, what do you do?

A Bunny Manual for trainees set guidelines and prohibitions in granular detail ("Bunnies are forbidden to date employees of the Club, including managers, room directors, bartenders, musicians, performers, busboys"). Fraternizing with members or guests would be cause for "immediate dismissal." The Club hired detectives to pose as customers who asked for a date or left a pair of theater tickets on a drinks tray. If she said "yes" to the date or scooped up the tickets, she must turn in her cottontail, a Bunny no more.

Trainees' speech and posture were keys to performance. The Training Bunny taught the rules for approaching the table "with a warm, welcoming smile. . . . when she reaches the table, she pivots gracefully and 'tails' the table. She should now be in her 'Bunny' Stance." Hefner's brother, Keith, who had studied at Lee Strasberg's famed Actors Studio, produced a film on "stylized serving techniques." The reel taught "such signature moves as the 'Bunny Stance,' the 'Bunny Dip,' the 'High Carry,' the 'Bunny Crouch,' and the 'Bunny Perch.'" Each must be mastered, for instance, the 'Dip,' performed when serving drinks and requiring "a graceful backward arch with knees together . . . to keep the girl's overstuffed, overextended breasts from popping out of the costume." "To motivate a proper state of mind before starting a shift," recalls Scott, "we were told to take a moment to think . . . a positive thought, then enter the room as though we were walking on stage."

So many Bunnies, so many specializations: Door Bunny, Cigarette Bunny, Camera Bunny (for photos at the table), Coat Check Bunny, Floor Bunny, Fine Dining Bunny—each of whom must memorize the cocktail menu and help bartenders with finishing touches when duty called. Each Bunny "learned to garnish twenty cocktail variations (sours, slings, collins, martinis, Manhattans, sidecars, gimlets"). Scott met the requirement to identify "31 Scotches, 16 bourbons, and 30 liqueurs."

Feminist Gloria Steinem briefly donned ears and tail to denounce the sexist Playboy Clubs for exploiting hapless female *naifs*, but Steinem's "A Bunny's Tale" in *Show* magazine (a two-part 1984 scathing essay on the seedy side of Bunnydom) might appear premature in light of Scott's roundup of Bunnies' impressive careers once they took leave of the Playboy Clubs. Their afterlives became a roster of professional achievement: a clinical social worker; an interior designer; vice president of a major cosmetics firm; medical transcriptionist; owner of clothing boutiques; currency trader; restaurateur; options market trader; real-estate "tycoon." Occasional reunions brought stories and laughter, but doubtless recollections too, from the Bunny "Dip" to the drink list every Bunny was required to "Commit to Memory," with the instruction to "place garnish on a Playboy pick."

GRASSHOPPER COCKTAIL

Ingredients:
1. ¾ ounce crème de cocoa
2. ¾ ounce crème de menthe
3. ¾ ounce heavy cream

Directions:
1. Fill shaker with ample ice.
2. Add all ingredients, shake vigorously, strain into cocktail glass, and serve.

TOM COLLINS

Ingredients:
1. 2–2½ ounces gin
2. 1–2 teaspoons sugar
3. ½–1 ounce lemon juice
4. Soda water
5. 1 slice lemon or orange (optional)
6. Maraschino cherry (optional)

Directions:
1. Fill shaker with ice.
2. Add gin, sugar, and lemon juice.
3. Strain into tall 14-ounce glass filled halfway with ice.
4. Add soda water, stir, and garnish to taste.

CUBA LIBRE COCKTAIL

Ingredients:
1. 1 ounce light rum
2. ½ ounce 151-proof rum
3. ½ ounce Coca-Cola
4. ½ ounce lime juice
5. ½ teaspoon sugar
6. Lime peel

Directions:
1. Fill shaker with ample ice.
2. Add both rums and all other ingredients.
3. Strain into prechilled cocktail glass.
4. Twist lime peel above drink and drop into glass.

GIBSON

Ingredients:
1. 2 ounces gin
2. ½ ounce dry vermouth
3. Cocktail onion

Directions:
1. Add ample ice to mixing glass.
2. Add gin and vermouth.
3. Strain and serve in prechilled cocktail glass.
4. Garnish with cocktail onion.

MARGARITA

Ingredients:
1. 1½ ounces tequila
2. ½ ounce Cointreau or triple sec
3. ½ ounce lemon or lime juice

Directions:
1. Rim cocktail glass with salt.
2. Add ample ice to shaker.
3. Add all ingredients and shake well.
4. Strain and serve.

OLD FASHIONED
Ingredients:
1. 1½ ounces blended whiskey
2. 1 or 2 dashes Angostura bitters
3. ½ teaspoon sugar
4. 1 teaspoon water
5. Lemon peel

Directions:
1. Stir sugar, water, and bitters in prechilled Old Fashioned glass until sugar dissolves.
2. Fill glass with hard, clear ice cubes or chunks.
3. Add whiskey.
4. Stir well.
5. Twist lemon peel above glass, drop it into drink, and serve.

ROB ROY
Ingredients:
1. 1½ ounces scotch whisky
2. ½ ounce sweet vermouth
3. 1 dash orange bitters

Directions:
1. Put ample ice in mixing glass.
2. Add whisky, vermouth, and bitters.
3. Stir well and strain into prechilled cocktail glass.

SIDECAR

Ingredients:
1. ¾ ounce brandy
2. ¾ ounce Cointreau or triple sec
3. ¾ ounce lemon juice

Directions:
1. Put ample in shaker.
2. Add all ingredients and shake well.
3. Strain into prechilled cocktail glass and serve.

WHISKEY SOUR

Ingredients:
1. 1½ ounces blended whiskey
2. ¾ ounce lemon juice
3. 1 teaspoon sugar
4. ½ slice lemon
5. 1 maraschino cherry

Directions:
1. Put ample ice in shaker.
2. Add whiskey, lemon juice, sugar, and shake well.
3. Strain into prechilled Whiskey Sour glass.
4. Garnish with lemon slice and cherry and serve.

IRISH COFFEE

Ingredients:
1. 5 or 6 ounces strong black coffee
2. 1½ ounces Irish whiskey
3. 1 teaspoon sugar
4. Sweetened whipped cream

Directions:
1. Preheat 8-ounce Irish Coffee glass or thick goblet.

2. Pour coffee and whiskey into goblet or glass.
3. Add sugar and stir until dissolved.
4. Add generous dollop of whipped cream to top and serve.

PINK LADY

Ingredients:
1. 1½ ounces gin
2. ¼ ounce lime juice
3. 1 teaspoon grenadine
4. ½ egg white
5. 1 teaspoon heavy cream

Directions:
1. Sugar-frost rim of cocktail glass.
2. Add ample ice to shaker.
3. Add ingredients and shake well.
4. Strain and serve.

✳ *8* ✳

JET SET

Come Fly with Me
—Frank Sinatra album, 1958
(title song by Jimmy Van Heusen and Sammy Cahn)

"Come fly with me, let's fly, let's fly away," crooned the legendary Frank Sinatra as gleaming passenger jets marked the newest aviation milestone that both expanded and shrank the globe. *Come Fly with Me* promised a magic carpet to float and glide in "rarified" air with nary a bumpy air pocket recollected from pre-jet days, while the tune's exotic destinations became jet-set bywords—Acapulco, Peru, Bombay. In 1958, the new Boeing 707 and Douglas DC-8 ferried passengers to those and other far-flung overseas locales and jetted them coast-to-coast in record time in planes painted with the logos of Pan American and National Airlines. The following year, American, Delta, and United offered jet service, and other airlines followed, although competition and mergers over decades would leave Eastern, Northwest, Braniff, and other airlines to aviation history.

Come Fly with Me invited highfliers to a special Bombay (now Mumbai) bar that served "exotic booze," but air travelers had long needed stiff drinks to muster courage to motor thousands of feet above *terra firma* on the strength of propellers whirling like hummingbirds' wings. Airport cocktail bars routinely fueled preflight passengers, but postwar years

identified "secret distresses," as sociologist Vance Packard termed Americans' anxieties about banks, overindulgence in sweets—and air travel. Businessmen and a few others had flown since the thirties but now airlines also sought couples, friends, and families in an expansive postwar moment of leisure travel to flourish only in a "psychologically calm environment." Airplane mishaps were few, but assuaging the anxious became the business plan, and pilots were drafted for voice training to instill confidence in the cabin. The airlines demanded "a voice that exudes confidence . . . pilots who can talk over the loud-speaker like they could fly an airplane . . . [and] talk with the voice of authority from the flight deck." Flight skill was rule *numero uno*, but filling the seats at thirty thousand feet required Captain Courageous at the mic.

From the postwar years, airlines also relied on "air hostesses" trained in reassurance that "all was well." Trainees practiced "talking in a calm, soft manner into tape recorders and listened to the playbacks of their voices for correction." Should passengers notice "sparks flying from an engine" in pre-jet aircraft, not to worry, for uniformed hostesses cooed airborne lullabies.

The airline "hostess" soon became a "stewardess," shortened to "stew," and bright young women from the hinterlands who felt tied down with humdrum boyfriends in Amarillo or Louisville, for instance, jumped at the career opportunity outlined in a 1958 vocational career guidebook for "airline hostess (Stewardess): *The main advantage is the opportunity to travel and see new places. The main disadvantage is being away from home at least a third of the time.*" Proclaimed Trudy Baker and Rachel Jones, "Therein lies the prime motivation to become a stewardess."

Baker and Jones's *Coffee, Tea, or Me?*, an insiders' tell-all memoir of careers as "stews," sparked a popular TV movie and became a bestseller and a catchphrase for an airborne working woman whom passengers called "Hey, Lady" or "Hey, Waitress." (Truth be told, the book was penned by an American Airlines PR man, Donald Bain, while "Trudy" and "Rachel" were Eastern Airlines "stews" posing as authors.)

Coffee, Tea, or Me? defined jet-set life from the ground up, starting with training that screened out young women ill-equipped to tangle with cranky adults and whining children, and unlikely to pour drinks like a skilled airborne bartender, let alone serve full-course meals under the tightest schedules or fend off self-styled Lotharios or execute emergency safety procedures on the instant—all the while modeling the latest stylish uniform and endlessly smiling in facial makeup worthy of a cosmetics counter makeover, plus high heels, nylon stockings, and a requisite girdle. (Midcentury "stews" met strict requirements for weight, and "never has a ruling caused so much controversy as with those airlines that retire girls at

thirty-two," while "anti-marriage rules forced many girls to hide the fact that they are married.")

A backward glance at midcentury jet-set dining shows an enchanted scene from an airborne Brigadoon. All passengers enjoyed cocktails and full-course meals while flying, for example, from a US city to the Caribbean or Hawaii, a five-hour flight the "stew" duo chronicled from takeoff: "We prepare and serve two hundred sixty diverse drinks, all from the liquor cart designed to fit in the aisle, not to function as a bar-on-wheels." Apologies to the "irate" passenger informed that mint juleps were not on offer or that the "premixed martini" wasn't dry enough, though soon everyone was offered a refreshing hot towel in preparation for the meal. Towels collected, the meal service began, and the "stews" apologized yet again that the steak might not be quite rare enough . . . or medium . . . or well-done. Perhaps the passenger would enjoy the dessert. ("And I'll bet your mother did make better apple pie.")

From passenger and "stew," delectable dining was a matter of record, as with college student and future author Joan Didion, who flew from her native California to New York in pre-jet 1955 but remembered her dinner and drinks six decades later, the "Beltsville Roast Turkey with Dressing and Giblet Sauce" and a return flight's "Martini-on-the-Rocks and Stuffed Celery au Roquefort." Former Eastern Airlines' jet-setting stewardess Jeanne Webb elaborates: "We served meals from famous restaurants with flowers, sterling silver, crystal, and china plates. . . . We served it in courses—the appetizers, salads and rolls, entrées, and desserts. There was plenty of champagne and wine to go with the meals," she recalled, and "sometimes people had a choice of steak or lobster," if not "roast beef and chicken." (One "stew" feared she might be fired: "They caught me stealing a lobster tail.")

Following after-dinner drinks, passengers often visited the cockpit. Recalled Webb, "The captain would make an announcement and invited the passengers up to the cockpit. . . . When they come back, we see them smiling and talking to everyone. . . . The children were thrilled because the captain talked to them and put his hat on their heads."

"Stews" frequently brought coffee and snacks up front to the pilot, copilot, and navigator, and flight crews from the cockpit to the cabin gelled as teams. Pride in one's own airline fostered tribal solidarity, and *Coffee, Tea, or Me?* profiled various airlines' "stews" in borderline critiques, such as the TWA "girls that have an air about them," while United settled for "average . . . middle-of-the-road in every way." The National Airlines stewardess showed "a hard look . . . a knowing look of sex, too knowing for other airlines," while Air Canada "likes plump, British-looking girls." Delta's are "Southern," and "Pan-Am's girls are primarily the snobby, jet-set type."

Competing for passengers, the airlines initially uniformed their stewardesses in quasi-military garb, but the new aerial atmosphere called for style when "jet set" defined a generation of sophisticates eager for travel that folded flight time into the overall leisure experience. In the early 1960s, couturier Emilio Pucci outfitted the Braniff International Airlines "Air Hostesses" in colorful knee-length, zip-front cocktail dresses and patterned stockings ("Introducing the Air Strip," teased the ad). Braniff also hired advertising genius Mary Wells to launch "The End of the Plain Plane" campaign, which turned each "staid" Braniff fuselage a bright turquoise, baby blue, medium blue, or lemon yellow, though lavender was discontinued because the color was considered bad luck south of the US border. (Pucci also designed clear plastic "space helmets" to fit over stews' bouffant hairstyles for unavoidable short walks when it rained.)

Vacationers jetted, but business counted on schedules that sped executives from site to site in record time. Wed to Braniff chief Harding Lawrence, Mary Wells Lawrence (b. 1928) set a pace possible only in the jet age. As founder and CEO of Wells Rich Greene, the booming advertising agency listed on Wall Street, Mary summed up her whirlwind days: "One minute I was in Rome, the next I was walking through real estate in downtown Dallas looking for a site for our new branch office and the next I was eyeing a building in Newport Beach to house the Century 21 account. Then, suddenly, there I was . . . at Ford World Headquarters." (The Wells Rich Greene agency captured the Ford corporate account.)

Business jet-setting found executive men cutting deals at renowned golf courses such as California's Pebble Beach or Torrey Pines. The rare midcentury female CEO upped the ante hosting clients in the south of France, where Mary Wells Lawrence and her husband bought a seafront villa near Monaco, home of former film star Princess Grace. "The men running other agencies may have been bonding with their clients while chasing little white balls around," recounted the CEO of Wells Rich Greene in her memoir, but "I bonded with my clients and their wives at La Fiorentina." They came for lengthy visits, she recalled, and bathed in the sea, sunned themselves, and were served dinners "in the pavilion by the sea." Sometimes, "Princess Grace of Monaco would come to dinner with my clients. . . . She would smile and rest her lovely eyes on the men and they would forget everyone else. Their wives never minded." At the end of the evening, CEO hostess Mary admitted, "I thought of my male competitors on their golf courses, and I laughed . . . to myself."

The famous and infamous jetted in these years, and the "stews" recognized notables who had flown with them. Eastern Airlines' Jeanne Webb recalled serving Eleanor Roosevelt, heart surgeon Michael DeBakey, opera star Luciano Pavarotti, Ted Williams of baseball fame, comedian Bob Hope, and Richard Nixon. Most memorable on "four different flights" was the "lovely . . . extremely beautiful" film star Elizabeth Taylor, who always made time for a conversation. ("On one flight she actually brought her own lunch because she had arrived a bit late, and she felt that we might not have enough food for late travelers.") Trudy and Rachel's extensive list of prominent jet-setters includes Duke Ellington, Johnny Carson, the "delightful" Lucille Ball, and Elizabeth Taylor with Richard Burton, both of whom "sat quietly . . . never asking for anything" but signed autographs to "the nicest stews we've ever traveled with."

Jet-setters' cocktails and other *de rigueur* drinks wend their way through memoirs of flights both domestic and international. On charters, "the liquor is poured in cascades," and otherwise the tally includes the double bourbons, the scotch on the rocks, the "Jacque Denielles" the "Virgin Marie's," the "Collins," the "stinger," and countless Martinis. The Caribbean routes to San Juan, Aruba, Trinidad, Barbados, the Dominican Republic, St. Thomas, Jamaica, and Mexico quickened tastes for the tequila and rum drinks abounding onshore and in resorts' swimming pool bars where vacationers swam up to the bar for drinks.

JACK DANIEL'S (ON THE ROCKS)

Ingredients:
1. 1½ ounces Jack Daniel's Old Number 7 whiskey
2. Cubed or chunked ice

Directions:
1. Put 3–4 cubes or equivalent ice into Old Fashioned glass.
2. Pour in whiskey and serve.

VIRGIN MARY COCKTAIL

Ingredients:
1. 6–8 ounces tomato juice
2. Worcestershire sauce

3. Tabasco sauce
4. ½ teaspoon horseradish (optional)
5. Celery stalk with leaves
6. Salt and pepper
7. Green olives (optional)

Directions:
1. Pour tomato juice in tall glass or mug with 6–7 ice cubes.
2. Add 2–3 dashes Worcestershire and one dash Tabasco sauce (and horseradish if desired).
3. Stir vigorously.
4. Add salt and pepper to taste.
5. Garnish with celery stalk so leaves overtop rim.
6. Olives may be added, speared with wood pick.

STINGER COCKTAIL

Ingredients:
1. 2 ounces cognac
2. 1 ounce white crème de menthe

Directions:
1. Add cognac and crème de menthe to mixing glass with ample ice.
2. Stir vigorously, strain into rocks glass filled with crushed ice, and serve.

ACAPULCO COCKTAIL

Ingredients:
1. 1½ ounces light rum
2. ¼ ounce triple sec
3. ½ ounce lime juice
4. ½ egg white

5. ½ teaspoon sugar
6. 2 fresh mint leaves

Directions:

1. Fill shaker with ice.
2. Add all ingredients except mint to shaker and shake vigorously.
3. Strain into cocktail glass and garnish with mint leaves slightly torn.

BACARDI COCKTAIL

Ingredients:

1. 1½ ounces light or golden Bacardi rum
2. ½ ounce lime juice
3. 1 teaspoon grenadine

Directions:

1. Fill shaker with ice.
2. Add all ingredients and shake well.
3. Strain into prechilled cocktail glass or over rocks in Old Fashioned glass.

CARIB COCKTAIL

Ingredients:

1. 1 ounce light rum
2. 1 ounce gin
3. ½ ounce lime juice
4. 1 teaspoon sugar
5. 1 slice orange

Directions:

1. Fill shaker with ice.
2. Add all ingredients except orange and shake vigorously.

3. Strain over rocks in Old Fashioned glass.
4. Garnish with orange slice and serve.

BEACHCOMBER COCKTAIL
Ingredients:
  1. 1½ ounces light rum
  2. ½ ounce lime juice
  3. ½ ounce triple sec
  4. ¼ ounce maraschino liqueur
Directions:
  1. Fill shaker with ice.
  2. Add all ingredients and shake vigorously.
  3. Strain into sugar-rimmed cocktail glass and serve.

EL PRESIDENTE COCKTAIL
Ingredients:
  1. 1½ ounces golden rum
  2. ½ ounce dry vermouth
  3. 1 teaspoon dark Jamaican rum
  4. 1 teaspoon curaçao
  5. 2 teaspoons lime juice
  6. ¼ teaspoon grenadine
Directions:
  1. Fill shaker with ice.
  2. Add all ingredients and shake vigorously.
  3. Strain into cocktail glass and serve.

OCHO RIOS COCKTAIL
Ingredients:
  1. 1½ ounces Jamaican rum
  2. 1 ounce guava nectar

3. 1½ ounces heavy cream
4. ½ ounce lime juice
5. ½ ounce sugar
6. ⅓ cup crushed ice

Directions:
1. Put all ingredients into electric blender.
2. Blend at low speed 10–15 seconds.
3. Pour into deep-saucer cocktail glass and serve.

PUERTO RICAN PINK LADY

Ingredients:
1. 1¾ ounces golden rum
2. 1 teaspoon grenadine
3. ¾ ounces lemon juice
4. ½ egg white
5. ⅓ cup crushed ice

Directions:
1. Put all ingredients into electric blender.
2. Blend at low speed 10–15 seconds.
3. Pour into sugar-rimmed deep-saucer champagne glass and serve.

PORT ANTONIO COCKTAIL

Ingredients:
1. 1 ounce golden rum
2. ½ ounce dark Jamaican rum
3. ½ ounce coffee liqueur
4. 1 teaspoon falernum (a Caribbean syrup)
5. 1 slice lime

Directions:
1. Fill shaker with ample ice.

2. Add all rum, lime juice, coffee liqueur, and falernum.
3. Shake vigorously, strain over rocks in Old Fashioned glass.
4. Garnish with lime slice and serve.

TEQUILA SOUR COCKTAIL

Ingredients:
1. 2 ounces tequila
2. ½ ounce lemon juice
3. 1 teaspoon sugar
4. ½ slice lemon
5. Maraschino cherry

Directions:
1. Fill shaker with ample ice.
2. Add all ingredients except cherry.
3. Shake vigorously, strain into Whiskey Sour glass, garnish with cherry, and serve.

DARK AND STORMY

Ingredients:
1. 2 ounces dark rum
2. ½ ounce fresh lime juice
3. 4–6 ounces ginger beer

Directions:
1. Add 4–5 ice cubes to tall glass or mug.
2. Add rum and lime juice.
3. Fill to brim with ginger beer.
4. Stir gently, garnish with lime slice, and serve.

JAMAICA ELEGANCE

Ingredients:
1. 1½ ounces Appleton's Jamaican rum
2. ½ ounce brandy
3. ½ ounce pineapple juice
4. 1 ounce fresh lime juice
5. 1 teaspoon simple syrup
6. Lime slice

Directions:
1. Fill shaker with ice.
2. Add all ingredients except lime slice and shake well.
3. Strain into 12-ounce glass and add ice to glass.
4. Stir gently, garnish with lime slice, and serve.

9

TIKI TIME

Polynesia: *n*. a scattered group of islands in the Pacific.
—*Webster's New World Dictionary*, 1964

Tahiti to Fiji, the far-flung islands challenged ancient naviga-
tors in outrigger canoes and machine-age heirs in steamships,
but the islands took America by storm when a midcentury
tsunami of Pacific treasures washed into American cities and
towns. From the West Coast to the heartland and the far-
thest Atlantic shores, an ambience of sugar white beaches and
palm trees, sun, surf, coconuts, tropical flowers, birds, and
exotic drinks sipped from a calabash or coconut shell—all
was summed up into one word, Polynesia. America labeled
the sixty million oceanic square miles the "South Pacific" and
nicknamed the Polynesian never-never land in one word: tiki.
A new world of libations for a thirsty America, tiki time meant
wondrous exotic flavors in an atmosphere of distant lands
where Martinis or scotch on the rocks made way for blissful
tiki drinks in a time out of time.

How a wood or stone image of a Polynesian supernatural
power, tiki, captivated midcentury America is a tale featuring
entrepreneurs and consumers from the 1930s Depression, the
WWII years of Pacific warfare, and the Broadway smash hit
and Hollywood film *South Pacific*. A tiki-mad USA, however,
traced its deeper roots to the perennial yearnings for leisure in
a country that hammered the virtue of work and eyed leisure

as a moral failing. Ingrained in the nation's DNA, hard work was promoted in such 1800s titles as *Strive and Succeed* by the prolific Horatio Alger, and generations of school pupils memorized "The Village Blacksmith," a verse commending the relentless day job of the "smithy" who toils at his anvil "week in, week out, from morn till night."

Fewer heard the voices promoting leisure, such as the poet Walt Whitman (b. 1819), whose "Song of Myself" begins, "I loafe and invite my soul / I lean and loafe at my ease." The loafing bard had company in the popular Scottish writer Robert Louis Stevenson (b. 1850), whose "An Apology for Happy Idlers" spoke for itself, while his songster in "The Vagabond" asks only for "the heaven above / And the road below me." Exponent of leisure, the idealized vagabond became the next century's envied American as Jack London (b. 1876) and Jack Kerouac hit the road, and hoboes were idealized for easygoing days hopping freight trains and camping under the stars. Folk and country balladeers celebrated leisure-in-transit in such tunes as Roger Miller's "King of the Road" (though Joan Baez later reprised the lament of a hard worker who could only dream of a "Rainbow Road").

The fantasy of leisure off the grid began in earnest when an itinerant merchant seaman and Prohibition bootlegger found his footing as the owner of a popular Hollywood bar that he named Don's Beachcomber. The self-fashioned Donn Beach had begun life as Ernest Gannt (b. 1907), and his confected life story includes a faithful son's help managing his mother's central Texas boardinghouses before visions of seagoing life drew him to saltwater ports of call. The young Texan crewed on vessels bound for Australia by way of Hawaii, and he claimed to have spent a few years island-hopping in the

South Pacific before settling in Los Angeles where he opened Ernie's Place, a speakeasy that pegged him as a bootlegger. Prohibition's end in 1933 prompted a fresh start when Ernest Gannt became Donn Beach, and by 1937 his bar expanded into a restaurant with the slightly altered name of Don the Beachcomber. America's tiki time had begun.

"If you can't get to paradise, I'll bring it to you," promised Don the Beachcomber with décor promoting fantasies of faraway tropical islands—a welcome escape in the

Depression years. Motifs of bamboo, driftwood, and rattan meshed with materials salvaged from Hollywood movie sets. A soundtrack of rain pattering on the roof, together with chopsticks and free souvenir leis let patrons imagine themselves as ex-pats dining on exotic fare and imbibing native drinks on a South Sea Island. In truth, the kitchen prepared the Cantonese foods familiar in Chinese restaurants but renamed "South Seas" selections. From the bar, however, Donn Beach is credited with launching the tiki genre of rum-based drinks, including the Zombie, Aku Aku, and Tahitian Rum Punch. Imbibing notables included Marlene Dietrich, Clark Gable, Vivien Leigh, Bing Crosby, and others. Donn's second wife, Sunny Sund, an adroit businesswoman, expanded Don the Beachcomber to a national chain of sixteen restaurants, its Chicago location especially successful. The former Ernest Gannt, meanwhile, created a "Polynesian Village" in Encino, California, where he hosted luaus for celebrities.

To the north, industrial Oakland set the stage for another Gold Rush à la Polynesia when a semi-disabled son of San Francisco's impoverished Mission District gambled on a dive bar that eventually expanded into a worldwide restaurant chain known as Trader Vic's. A friendly rival of Donn Beach, this "P. T. Barnum of the restaurant world" was to give all America its tiki time-out in a carefully crafted Polynesia.

Known in boyhood as "Little Vicky," the future self-styled Trader Vic—Victor J. Bergeron (b. 1902)—survived a hardscrabble childhood beset with ills and the loss of a leg, which put him on crutches for years. His French Canadian immigrant parents opened a small grocery in Oakland, a family business that employed their son, who began to see opportunity in a

nearby vacant lot. Victor's brief stint in a business college and a borrowed $500 for a carpentered shack on the lot launched the 1934 beer hall he named Hinky Dink's. Hustler Vic's instincts paid off when Hinky Dink's became a successful "social club" despite the Depression—or precisely because the economic downturn was ripe for gatherings for the fun of it. The local Hinky Dink's crowd loved Vic's "gimmicks and giveaways," such as the five o'clock "free lunch" or the microphone set up for "amateur night." To offset Oakland's bone-chilling drafts, Vic began to "insulate" with solid objects hung on the thin wood walls. Recounts biographer Steve Siegelman, "Within a year every inch of the walls and ceiling was lined with antlers, animals, shotguns, horseshoes, snowshoes, and sideshow oddities." Vic found that "lots of decoration causes lots of conversation, and lots of conversation sells lots of drinks." Hinky Dink's boomed, and the thirty-four-year-old Vic Bergeron tasted success.

The route to Trader Vic's started with suspicion that the future did not belong to a "grog and chow" outlet like Hinky Dink's, but to a different drinking and dining experience as the country eased out of the Depression. With his wife, Esther, Vic sought ideas in the Caribbean, in New Orleans, and in San Francisco's Chinatown. He experimented with rum-based drinks, and he toured island-themed bars and restaurants, including Don the Beachcomber in Southern California. The idea of the tropics writ large in a restaurant took hold, though the trifling name, Hinky Dink's, had to go. "My wife suggested Trader Vic's," recalled the ambitious Victor Bergeron, "because I was always making a trade with someone," and because "the place should be named after someone we could tell a story about."

Spinning life stories fit the Polynesian myth, and Trader Vic was soon rumored to have begun life on "a tiny island in the South Pacific," his leg lost in a shark attack. "What exactly did he trade in? Fur? Rum?" Guesswork fed the myth, but feeding (and hydrating) customers required careful planning. Vic had tinkered with mixed drinks and studied bartenders' guides, but a crash course in rums produced new concoctions, such as Tonga Punch, Fog Cutter, and the Outrigger Tiara. To overhaul the menu, Chinese cooks in the Trader Vic's kitchen produced dishes already favored on the West Coast but tweaked to sound Polynesian. The Trader Vic's Tiki Bar would feature Crab Rangoon, Po Po, and Trader's Oven Smoked Morsels, but also hamburgers and steak sandwiches served in a totally

revamped interior. "Up went enough tapa cloth and thatch to build a new Polynesian village," and drinks and food arrived in "South Seas-style ceramic vessels . . . from giant Kava bowls and rum kegs to skull-shaped mugs for hot-buttered rum," each one a Trader Vic's "signature," as were tropical flowers and souvenir swizzle sticks. The former Hinky Dink's was reborn in 1937 as Trader Vic's.

The explosive expansion of Trader Vic's restaurants began with its second location in San Francisco and WWII, which brought fame's high tide when the patriotic Vic Bergeron "hydrated" US troops with care packages dispatched to the South Pacific. "California restaurant's fancy rum drinks are famous in the South Seas," bannered a 1944 headline in pictorial *Life* magazine, which featured Trader Vic's tiki ceramics and sailors sipping an exotic cocktail. The Polynesian state of mind continued into the postwar and midcentury years that saw the restaurant chain expand in tandem with popular culture. The Weston and Hilton hotels featured Trader Vic's in Denver, Chicago, Boston, New York, Vancouver, Kansas City, Atlanta, and overseas in Tokyo, London, Munich, and elsewhere. Meanwhile, writer James Michener won the Pulitzer Prize for the 1948 bestseller *Tales of the South Pacific*, which became the basis for the Broadway musical and Hollywood film starring Rossano Brazzi and Mitzi Gaynor. The musical's Rodgers and Hammerstein hit song "Bali Hai" was covered by Peggy Lee and others, and a TV series of 1959, *Adventures in Paradise*, broadcast images of yachting in the Islands, while Michener's bestselling novel *Hawaii* sparked interest, and the movie *Blue Hawaii*, starring Elvis Presley, put the North Pacific island chain into the South Pacific, which most Americans liked just fine. The comedy series *Gilligan's Island* (1964–67) kept the country mindful of the uniqueness of faraway islands.

Numerous local restaurants across the country copied the Polynesian tiki format, including the Kowloon outside of Boston and Fort Lauderdale's Mai-Kai, which opened in 1956, calling itself "the longest-running Polynesian show in the United States, including Hawaii." One New York commuter rail outfitted a jungle tiki bar car for gray flannel–suited commuters, and *Trader Vic's Pacific Island Cookbook* and trademarked foods and mixes promoted Polynesia for backyard barbecues. By midcentury, the South Seas tiki had come home for good—an American idol.

MAI TAI (CLAIMED TO ORIGINATE AT DON THE BEACHCOMBER *AND* TRADER VIC'S)

Ingredients:
1. 3 ounces light rum
2. ¼ ounce triple sec
3. ¼ ounce orzata
4. ½ ounce lime juice
5. ½ teaspoon sugar
6. 1 slice lime
7. 1 sprig mint
8. 1 pineapple stick

Directions:
1. Fill shaker with ample ice.
2. Add rum, triple sec, orzata, and sugar.
3. Strain into double Old Fashioned glass.
4. Add enough cracked ice to fill glass.
5. Pinch mint leaves to release flavor and garnish with lime slice and pineapple stick.

ZOMBIE HIGHBALL

Ingredients:
1. 1 ounce light rum
2. 1 ounce dark rum
3. 1 ounce curaçao
4. ¼ ounce grenadine
5. 1½ ounces orange juice
6. 1 ounce lemon juice
7. ¼ ounce lime juice
8. 1 cup crushed ice
9. Mint sprig

Directions:
1. Add all ingredients except mint sprig to electric blender.
2. Pulse on low setting for 8–10 seconds.
3. Pour into highball glass, garnish with mint sprig, and serve.

TAHITIAN PUNCH (FOR THIRTY)
Ingredients:
1. 1 bottle white rum
2. 1 bottle dark rum
3. 2½ cups Grand Marnier
4. 3 quarts fresh orange juice
5. 3 quarts pineapple juice
6. 2 limes (quartered)
7. 1 teaspoon vanilla extract
8. 2½ cups simple syrup

Directions:
1. Mix all ingredients together.
2. Let stand at least 6 hours.
3. Remove lime quarters.
4. Pour mixture into punch bowl(s) and ladle each serving into a punch cup.

TONGA PUNCH
Ingredients:
1. 2 ounces light rum
2. ¼ ounce grenadine
3. ½ ounce curaçao
4. 1½ ounces fresh orange juice

5. ¾ ounce lemon juice
6. ¼ ounce lime juice
7. 1 cup crushed ice
8. Mint sprig

Directions:
1. Add all ingredients except mint sprig to electric blender.
2. Pulse on low setting for 8–10 seconds.
3. Pour into glass, garnish with mint sprig, and serve.

AKU AKU

Ingredients:
1. 1 ounce light rum
2. ½ ounce peach liqueur
3. ½ ounce lime juice
4. 4 chunks fresh pineapple
5. Several large mint leaves and 1 mint sprig
6. ½ teaspoon simple syrup
7. 1½ cups crushed ice

Directions:
1. Add all ingredients except mint sprig to electric blender.
2. Pulse on low setting for 15 seconds.
3. Pour into double Old Fashioned glass, garnish with mint sprig, and serve.

OUTRIGGER TIARA

Ingredients:
1. 1 ounce light rum
2. 1 ounce dark rum

3. 1 ounce fresh orange juice
4. 1 ounce lemon juice
5. 1 dash grenadine
6. 1 dash curaçao
7. 1½ cups crushed ice
8. Gardenia (for garnish)

Directions:
1. Add all ingredients except gardenia to electric blender.
2. Pulse on low setting for 8–10 seconds.
3. Pour over rocks into double Old Fashioned glass, garnish with gardenia, and serve.

BLUE HAWAIIAN (SPECIALTY OF THE ROYAL HAWAIIAN HOTEL, HONOLULU)

Ingredients:
1. 1½ ounces light rum
2. ½ ounce blue curaçao
3. 1 ounce coconut syrup
4. 3 ounces fresh pineapple juice
5. ¼ ounce lemon juice
6. 1½ cups crushed ice
7. 1 pineapple stick
8. Mint sprig

Directions:
1. Add all ingredients except pineapple stick and mint to electric blender.
2. Pulse on low setting 8–10 seconds.
3. Pour into double Old Fashioned glass, garnish with pineapple stick and mint, and serve.

GUN CLUB PUNCH

Ingredients:

1. 1 ounce light rum
2. 1 ounce dark rum
3. 1½ ounces unsweetened pineapple juice
4. ½ ounce lime juice
5. 1 dash grenadine
6. 1 dash curaçao
7. 1 cup crushed ice
8. 1 pineapple stick
9. Mint sprig

Directions:

1. Add all ingredients except pineapple stick and mint sprig to electric blender.
2. Pulse on low setting 8–10 seconds.
3. Pour into tumbler or highball glass, garnish with pineapple stick and mint, and serve.

FOG CUTTER

Ingredients:

1. 2 ounces light rum
2. 1 ounce brandy
3. ½ ounce gin
4. 2 ounces lemon juice
5. 1 ounce fresh orange juice
6. ½ ounce orgeat syrup
7. 1 cup crushed ice
8. ¼ ounce sherry
9. Mint sprig

Directions:
1. Put all ingredients except sherry and mint into cocktail shaker.
2. Shake vigorously.
3. Pour into double Old Fashioned glass and add cubed ice to fill glass.
4. Float sherry on top, garnish with mint sprig, and serve.

BOOMERANG COCKTAIL

Ingredients:
1. 1 ounce pisco brandy
2. 1 ounce light rum
3. ¾ ounce passion fruit syrup
4. ½ ounce lemon juice
5. Lemon twist for garnish

Directions:
1. Add ample ice cubes to shaker.
2. Add all ingredients except lemon twist.
3. Strain into cocktail glass, garnish with lemon twist, and serve.

10

BACHELOR PADS

A man's home . . . should be . . . an exciting expression of the person he is and the life he leads.
—"*Playboy*'s Penthouse Apartment," 1956

If you are to be a glamorous, sophisticated woman . . . you need an apartment and you need to live in it alone!
—Helen Gurley Brown, *Sex and the Single Girl*, 1962

America's bachelors, men and women committed to the city, took the spotlight in the postwar years to showcase a lifestyle unique to their time and place. While the midcentury suburbanite was hailed as a postwar pioneer, the bachelor and bachelor girl turned trailblazer with manners and mores that stamped the era with a new lifestyle that continued well into the future. Adopting the nickname "pad," the British slang term for an unmarried man's living space, the new singles generation turned thumbs down on suburban commutes and rejected fusty in-town rooming houses with kitchen privileges. They said "no" to roommates and, with all due respect to the ancestral home, refused to bunk in the bedrooms of their youth. Venturing into cityscapes of their own, they leased compact studio apartments and, if affordable, opted for lavish terraced penthouses. This bachelor generation sought personalized space in which to eat, sleep, drink, socialize, and entertain nightlong as the opportunities arose. They understood that knowledge of wines and liquors came with their territory, as did the correct glasses and barware and the nimble handling thereof.

Men's and women's bachelor pads were distinguished, inevitably, by midcentury's gendered "His" vs. "Hers." While a career girl concealed her bed, for example, her male counterpart might flaunt his "magnificent sleeping platform on veneer plywood and legs." At its best, the man's bachelor apartment mirrored the new space-age central command, where switches meant power and automation triumphed. The moneyed man's pad featured high-tech equipment, such as "silent mercury switches . . . that subtly dim the bedroom lighting to just the right romantic level." Throughout his apartment, "screens, speakers, and cooking implements were all controlled with the flip of a switch." A "glass-domed oven" in his kitchen space could roast "luscious viands in tantalizing view," the meal served by the host "in a sleekly modern, Scandinavian-style dining room."

Men relied heavily on *Playboy* magazine for tips on bachelor furnishings and entertainment. The magazine touted Eames chairs and a Noguchi table, preferably originals, though knockoffs would do on a taut budget. Leather sofas and low-slung lounge chairs were featured, and home accessories played in masculine counterpoint, the gaming table with the rack of briar pipes, the hi-fi sound system with long-playing jazz albums (Miles Davis, Dave Brubeck), together with a few books in handsome leather bindings.

A fully stocked bar, *de rigueur* for the bachelor, lent itself to his dominant image—as wolf. "When he was not inviting a woman to come up and see his etchings" (seduction's cliché of the era), he was "howling at her door." Whether the

bachelor was shy or outgoing, he was, at base, a wolf on the hunt, and his prowess at the bar showed the skillful hunter in the guise of a suave host. "Some hosts are content to offer a swig to their guests as long as it provides a passing sensation of alcohol in the body," a midcentury bar guide conceded, but *Playboy*'s food and wine guru, Thomas Mario, countered such crudity with connoisseurship: "Superb spirits and fine wines, like the best examples of the culinary arts, are carefully chosen, skillfully served, and remembered with vivid pleasure." Whether the libations were colorless gin and vodka, or tawny bourbon or scotch, wrote Mario, "you see in all of them a common element: their fascinating endless mixability."

Privileged midcentury bachelors had learned to mix drinks from observing family rituals in homes with well-stocked liquor cabinets. They had watched cocktails crafted at their families' country clubs or at exclusive clubs where their fore-fathers had been charter members. Countless midcentury bachelors, however, were rich in cash and credit cards, but neophytes at the bar and eager for *Playboy*'s crash course in the mysteries of mixology, which included a slightly satirical ten-step production of the "perfect martini." Rivaling the precision of laboratory bench chemistry, the 1955 Martini called for the gin and vermouth to be measured by the cubic centimeter and an olive sized by a caliper. ("Stir concoction no less than 25 revolutions. Wrist action is very important here.")

The *Playboy* bachelor was assured that with guidance (and skill honed in private), he could host a successful party or a quiet evening of drinking and dining "*intime*." Bar savant Mario endorsed the modern 4½-ounce cocktail glasses that replaced "parsimonious" 3-ounce glasses. "Not only does the larger cocktail provide more sumptuous bliss for guests, but it's a boon to the host since it means fewer refills and the coveted chance to sit down, drink, and enjoy the revels."

Playboy accorded the cocktail preeminence among drinks, but listed dos and don'ts for the bachelor:

1. Inferior liquors aren't masked in cocktails.
2. Don't imitate free-pouring bartenders. . . . Be mathematically accurate.
3. Ice must be hard, cold, and clean.
4. Anyone can begin shaking cocktails. An artist knows when to stop.
5. Use the proper glass for each cocktail and be sure it's sparkling clean and prechilled.
6. Use fresh ingredients in your cocktails, especially when it comes to fruit juices.

7. The stirred cocktail is clear; the shaken cloudy.
8. Make your own personal recipe changes only with the greatest care. Be creative if you will, but create slowly and deftly.

For the bachelor's party planning, a "Drink Calculator" advised that each guest would imbibe "two or three drinks at the usual cocktail hour at sundown," wines with dinner, and "two or three highballs after dinner," though the formula would expand to four-to-six at a "knock-down, drag-out bachelor party." Among the recommended cocktails: the Martini, Brandy Sour, Gimlet, and Applejack Manhattan.

* * *

The bachelor "single girl" paid little heed to the "Drink Calculator," since her social strategies differed radically from the vulpine male's tactics. Men had *Playboy*, but a bestseller for unmarried women burst from the gender divide in 1962 when Helen Gurley Brown published *Sex and the Single Girl*, a soup-to-nuts manual on turning a wolf into a husband and relishing the process every step of the way.

The daughter of an Arkansas homemaker and a political appointee father who died when she was ten years old, Helen Marie Gurley (b. 1922) was an unlikely candidate for midcentury media stardom. Horizons widened when her widowed mother took fifteen-year-old Helen and her older sister, Mary Eloine, to Los Angeles, where Helen attended the John H. Francis Polytechnic High School in Downtown LA. With diploma in hand, she joined her mother and sister in a move to Warm Springs, Georgia, where her polio-stricken sister received treatment. While Arkansas called her mother and sister home, Helen opted for LA. By 1941, she had logged one semester at Texas State College for Women and graduated from the Woodbury Business College in Los Angeles. Surefire clerical skills secured secretarial jobs at talent and advertising agencies, but Helen's adroit writing won promotions, raised her salary, and inspired *Sex and the Single Girl*. On the East Coast, bosses at a general-interest magazine with slumping sales took note of the book's blockbuster success, and Helen Gurley—now Helen Gurley Brown (Mrs. David Brown)—joined *Cosmopolitan* magazine in 1965. Editor-in-chief, she transformed "*Cosmo*" into shorthand for the magazine and the sexually liberated women who made "Single Girl" synonymous with "Sex."

Brown beamed her personal manifesto to single women who could never hope to be crowned Miss America or star in films: "I am not beautiful . . . not bosomy or brilliant. . . . I didn't go to college. . . . I'm an introvert and I am sometimes mean and cranky." Negatives aside, she had triumphed: "I married for the first time at thirty-seven. I got the man I wanted . . . a motion picture producer, forty-four, brainy, charming and sexy. . . . We have two Mercedes Benzes, one hundred acres of virgin forest near San Francisco, a Mediterranean house overlooking the Pacific, a full-time maid, and a good life."

If the virtuous "good life" failed to entice, the dazzling tally of riches made Brown's book a page-turner. A woman's "I do" at the altar, it insisted, must be postponed to free up time for the "best years" with men who are "often cheaper emotionally and a lot more fun by the dozen." The single girl, Brown proclaimed, was a working girl, gainfully employed and rigorously self-caring. To set her course, she must steer clear of the rocks and shoals of untimely marriage. ("It takes guts . . .

it can be lonely out there.") "Far from being a creature to be pitied and patronized," the single woman "is emerging as the newest glamor girl of our times."

The glamorizing took serious effort, and *Sex and the Single Girl* tapped into America's much-vaunted work ethic to detail the spinster's rigorous transformation into a playgirl. Her makeover began with an inventory of ambient men and where to meet them, from the bank teller's window to the ski slopes. (Pickups in bars were discouraged, as were married men unlikely to beeline to the divorce court, despite ardent promises of future nuptials with the single girl.) Cosmetics mattered, but sexiness was a practical matter of pros and cons. The aspirant glamor girl must eschew short hair, girdles, monologues about family and bosses, and a squeaky voice. On the sexy side, she must have clean hair, lovely lingerie, smiles, reasonably good health, perfume, a low voice, and "*The* black dress, the dress you paid more for than you should have but every time you wear it you feel bitchy and beautiful." And when a guy calls, "Light up!"

On its own terms, the single girl's seraglio must be as seductive as the bachelor man's *Playboy* penthouse, but a challenge loomed: how to pull it off on the slimmest fraction of a man's earnings. Brown's years as a working girl on a shoestring budget grounded her advice to single women who spent workdays in typing pools, at receptionists' desks, at classroom blackboards, or working nine-to-five in a raft of other poorly paid jobs believed to be just right for women. *Sex and the Single Girl* sang loud and clear to this demographic sisterhood. (Well-heeled singles were welcome to listen—and learn.)

A first principle dictated that a straitened budget must not crimp the single girl's safari for a man—for *him*. "Inexpensive"

and "cheap" were not synonyms. Brown's tips for finding and furnishing the single girl's apartment became a scout's guide into the urban forest. Were rents too high on the posh side of town? No matter. "Elegant apartments" can "gleam like pearls in crazy old neighborhoods." An unfurnished flat was creativity's opportunity to do it yourself with a fresh coat of paint, junk shop finds, and eclectic accessories that work wonders. A decorator, if affordable, could help, but good taste could be (and must be) cultivated. "Visit museums containing rooms of period furniture. . . . Borrow library books. . . . Immerse yourself in cherry wood and Chippendale." If a priceless Ming vase is out of reach, try "a crystal bowl of real apples and oranges catching the sun." "A chic apartment can tell the world that you, for one, are not one of those miserable, pitiful single creatures."

Under the heading "To Please a Man," Brown nevertheless tallied apartment must-haves, including travel posters, "gobs" of framed pictures, a "TV set," books, a hi-fi system, a "toga-size terry bath sheet" (for his showers in your apartment), and "a sexy kitchen," since "anything gadgety usually pleasures a male." A beautiful apartment, Brown's reader learned, "is a sure man-magnet."

Magnetic entertainment in *Sex and the Single Girl* ranged from cocktail parties to late-night dinners *à deux*, but the novice hostess earned her *"magna cum cookery"* by sharpening taste buds, paying "loving attention to detail," and gaining the confidence to serve one and all with brio. From a picnic to Sunday brunch to "DINNER *(for him)*," the recipes rolled from sauces, salad, and soufflés to the command performance of pricy lobster (*"en Brochette"* if not "stuffed tails").

Brown's "Care and Feeding of Everybody" cast a wide net but precisely advised the single girl about libations. Her man-of-the-moment could expect wine and/or liquor but was put on notice, as necessary, that her apartment was not "his friendly neighborhood bar with all the drinks on the house." (Her cue: "Charlie, darling . . . I think it would be a nice idea, since you adore Old Forester, if you brought a bottle over here with you next time.") To avoid bankruptcy when stocking booze, the single girl should rely on the liquor store dealer to point out which low-priced brands of bourbon and scotch were "potable." Her cocktail party need not require a bank loan if she circulated with several chilled pitchers of "weak" Martinis that create "a feeling of well-being and good fellowship in guests." For a Roman bacchanal of a dessert, Brown suggested a scoop of rich ice cream atop fresh fruit and dashes of each guest's chosen liqueur—"Grand Marnier,

Cointreau, crème de menthe." (Expensive, but the liqueurs "last for ages. . . . Hide them from your alcoholic friends.")

Helen Gurley Brown dubbed her favorite Sunday brunch beverage the "chloroform cocktail." Named for a notable anesthetic, her liquid *coup de grâce* would fell tall timber and saplings alike. "I remember," she confided, "one sweet girl who came over directly from church, had two chloroform cocktails because they tasted like coffee malteds and was still asleep (to put it euphemistically) under the coffee table at five in the afternoon."

Sex and the Single Girl kept clear of chloroform for the bachelor girl on the hunt for her man, but the midcentury single girl surfaces as huntress. The "wolves" shake seductive cocktails in their penthouse lairs, but the "newest glamor girl" is on the prowl for the "poor darling" she can snare. "Chill the cocktail glasses," Brown advises. "Don't postpone dinner indefinitely. He may be hungrier than you think." She counts on it!

HELEN GURLEY BROWN CHLOROFORM COCKTAILS

Ingredients:
1. Six 8-ounce cups coffee
2. One "fifth" gin or vodka
3. 1 quart rich vanilla ice cream
4. Nutmeg

Directions:
1. In saucepan, reduce coffee to 1 cup.
2. In large bowl, mix coffee with gin or vodka and ice cream.
3. Fill pilsner or Old Fashioned glasses with mixture.
4. Top with grated nutmeg and serve (serves 4).

PIERCINGLY COLD 8-TO-1 MARTINI

Ingredients:
1. 2 ounces gin
2. ¼ ounce dry vermouth
3. Pitless small olive

Directions:
1. Refrigerate gin and vermouth.
2. Put several rock-hard, clear ice cubes into prechilled mixing glass.
3. Add gin and vermouth.
4. Energetically stir with the ice.
5. Strain into prechilled cocktail glass, add olive, and serve.

BRANDY SOUR

Ingredients:
1. 2 ounces brandy
2. ½ ounce lemon juice
3. ¼ ounce orange juice
4. ½–1 teaspoon sugar
5. ½ slice lemon

Directions:
1. In ice-filled shaker, add all ingredients except lemon slice.
2. Shake vigorously.
3. Strain into prechilled Whiskey Sour glass, garnish with lemon slice, and serve.

GIMLET

Ingredients:

1. 2 ounces gin
2. ½ ounce Rose's lime juice

Directions:

1. Moisten prechilled cocktail glass rim with Rose's lime juice and dip rim in sugar.
2. Put ample ice into prechilled mixing glass.
3. Add gin and Rose's lime juice.
4. Stir thoroughly and completely.
5. Strain into cocktail glass and serve.

APPLEJACK MANHATTAN

Ingredients:

1. 1¾ ounces applejack
2. ¾ ounce sweet vermouth
3. 1 dash orange bitters
4. 1 maraschino cherry

Directions:

1. Put ample ice in mixing glass.
2. Add applejack, vermouth, and bitters.
3. Stir well and strain into prechilled cocktail glass.
4. Add cherry and serve.

11

BREAKFASTING AT TIFFANY'S

In his second novel, *Breakfast at Tiffany's* (1958), the celebrated author Truman Capote introduced his readers to a thoroughly modern American woman, a mysterious, irresistible creature who takes center stage in a novel about self-fashioning, resilience, fragility, improvisation, and wanderlust. In the process he created an icon.

Named Truman Persons at his birth in New Orleans on September 30, 1924, the young boy was reared by his mother's relatives in Monroeville, Alabama, until his divorced mother remarried in 1932, when he took his stepfather's name. While attending private prep schools in New York and New England, he made his name with stories in literary quarterlies and high-profile monthlies like *Mademoiselle* and *Harper's Bazaar* and at twenty-four years of age won the O. Henry Award with the story "Shut a Final Door." The openly gay Capote then created a literary sensation with his semiautobiographical first novel, *Other Voices, Other Rooms* (1948), a tale of family fracture set within a collapsing Alabama plantation house, a staple of the Southern Gothic tradition. Capote later worked in Hollywood and on Broadway, and virtually invented the genre of true crime with his bestselling account of the murder of a farm family in America's heartland, *In Cold Blood* (1965).

In *Breakfast at Tiffany's* Capote imagined an enigmatic young woman who sprinkles French phrases in conversation, calls assorted men "darling," and drinks for business, for pleasure, and for the cool nerve she needs to maintain her life's highwire act. The story, most of which takes place in the early 1940s during the war, is told from the point of view of a young writer who has moved into the flat above hers in a brownstone in the East Seventies on New York's Upper East Side.

Fascinated by her all-night hours, the new neighbor spots her one summer morning in the daylight, a sylph of "chic thinness" wearing a "slim cool black dress," black sandals, and a pearl choker. Her boyish "ragbag" short haircut and oversize dark glasses add an engaging fillip, and her "breakfast-cereal air of health" a wholesome touch. Two months shy of her nineteenth birthday, she might be a *Vogue* or *Harper's Bazaar* cover image of "consequential good taste." Her calling cards announce: "Miss Holiday Golightly, Traveling."

From a distance, the neighbor had already glimpsed Holly at swank Gotham clubs and watering holes surrounded by businessmen or "whiskey-eyed" military officers. The two neighbors frequently eye one another at Joe Bell's neighborhood bar where they take turns using the coin-operated telephone, but their friendship begins one late night when a rapping at the writer's window distracts him from a detective novel and bourbon nightcap. "I've got the most terrifying man downstairs," Holly gushes, stepping from the fire escape into his apartment through the opened window. "If there's one thing I loathe," she says, "it's men who bite. . . . I mean, he's sweet when he isn't drunk," but "eight martinis before dinner and enough wine to wash an elephant."

The "tiresome beast" would sleep it off in her apartment and go home, she felt sure. For now, she was one floor up, safe, and hungry. Eyeing a bowl of apples and her host's bourbon, she says, "Whiskey and apples go together. Fix me a drink, darling."

The elusive Holly is ever frank and yet evasive, specific but vague. Her livelihood, the friend learns, consists of nights spent with older men who tip well, together with lucrative weekly visits to Sing Sing prison to cheer up an old man who gives her a "weather report" she passes on to a mob-linked lawyer, oblivious of her legal peril and indifferent to the Mafia criminal snare that worries her new friend. Somehow, Tiffany & Co. figures in the story, not for its shopping, but for its solace, like a calm and serene chapel. (The 1961 film version, starring Audrey Hepburn, features Holly peering into Tiffany's window, browsing the hushed showroom floor, and shopping on a lark with her upstairs writer friend.) Throughout Capote's novella, Holly follows her wits and the guidance of her unique Holly-isms:

> "I'll never get used to anything. Anybody that does, they might as well be dead."
> "Any gent with the slightest chic will give you fifty for the girl's john."
> "I'd never be a movie star. It's too hard; and if you're intelligent, it's too embarrassing."
> "I don't want to own anything until I know I've found the place where me and things belong together."
> "Be anything but a coward, a pretender, an emotional crook, a whore."
> "You can make yourself love anybody."
> "I want to still be me when I wake up one fine morning and have breakfast at Tiffany's."

Capote's novel is awash in alcohol. Cocktails in Holly's apartment one night become a haphazard "stag party" of "strangers among strangers," probably because the hostess "had distributed her invitations while zigzagging through various bars." Among the guests: a rich playboy who mixes Martinis, and a Hollywood agent who sketches her mysterious past as a promising Hollywood starlet, infuriating her backers by decamping on the eve of her big screen test, just when they had invested in French lessons to "smooth out" her "hillbilly or Okie" voice and taught her to speak proper English. The agent, still smitten with his former protégé, swears Holly Golightly is "a *real* phony," an authentic version of the self she has created.

Joe Bell's bar finds the two friends frequently on hand, alternately to celebrate and commiserate their fates. The fledgling writer's first published short story calls for Manhattans to start the day, followed by "champagne cocktails on the house" when Joe hears the young man has broken into print. When Holly's sad past as a backwoods child bride surfaces, the friends touch glasses and drown sorrows over Joe's Martinis. When the plot thickens with Holly mired in a serious legal brouhaha, Joe shakes a "triple martini and a brandy tumbler full of coins" for the phone calls for a lawyer. His send-off gift is the airport limo that ferries Holly to a flight to Brazil, an escape from the law that Holly insists must include her century-old rare bottle of brandy.

Joe Bell serves Holly's friend one last time, twelve years later when new photographs surface, suggesting that Holly Golightly might be traveling in Africa, though neither man can be certain the photos are real. As Joe mixes the friend a White Angel cocktail, both admit to one certainty, that they are forever in love with Holly Golightly, having ignored the one Holly-ism they should have heeded themselves: "You can't give your heart to a wild thing."

WHITE ANGEL COCKTAIL
Ingredients:
1. 1½ or 2 ounces dry gin
2. 1½ or 2 ounces vodka
Directions:
1. Put gin and vodka in shaker.
2. Add ample cubed ice.
3. Shake, strain, and serve in chilled Martini glass.

MANHATTAN COCKTAIL

Ingredients:
1. 2 ounces rye whiskey
2. ¾ ounce sweet vermouth
3. 2 dashes Angostura bitters
4. Twist of orange peel

Directions:
1. Put first 3 ingredients in mixing glass with ample ice.
2. Stir thoroughly and strain into cocktail glass.
3. Garnish with orange peel.

MARTINI COCKTAIL

Ingredients:
1. 3 ounces dry gin
2. ½ ounce dry (white) vermouth
3. 2 unstuffed green olives

Directions:
1. Put ample ice in mixing glass.
2. Pour gin and vermouth over the ice.
3. Stir until gin and vermouth are very cold.
4. Strain into chilled cocktail glass.
5. Add olives and serve.

CHAMPAGNE COCKTAIL

Ingredients:
1. 3 ounces chilled champagne
2. ⅓ ounce cognac or brandy
3. 2 dashes Angostura bitters
4. 1 sugar cube
5. Maraschino cherry or orange slice

Directions:

1. Drop sugar cube into chilled champagne flute.
2. Carefully saturate sugar with bitters.
3. Add cognac.
4. Gently pour in champagne.
5. Garnish with cherry or orange slice and serve.

12

ISLANDS IN THE STREAM

The Gulf Stream beckoned "Papa" Ernest Hemingway as the oceans had lured writers before him. Their seafaring fiction promised adventure and exotic encounters in far-flung lands, but Hemingway (b. 1899) chose familiar salt seas and nearby islands to launch his new post-WWII project. Bimini and Cuba would loom large, both islands familiar from Prohibition's rum-running 1920s and thereafter open to tourists. In addition, the Caribbean of the 1930s and WWII would backstop the book-in-progress that was well underway in 1950 with a working title of "The Island and the Stream." Hemingway began the project as a "straightforward" novel that nonetheless turned "complex and introspective" over a period of fifteen years. Secured in a bank vault, the unpublished manuscript was retrieved after his death in 1961 and appeared as *Islands in the Stream*. His legacy lives in its three parts—"Bimini," "Cuba," "At Sea"—each evoking its immediate time and place, each lightened with drinks that steadied and sobered Hemingway's lead character, a figure much like "Papa" himself.

Thomas Hudson takes center stage in *Islands* as a successful seascape painter who, like the midlife Hemingway, is a divorced father of sons and will become a warrior when he sees action against the Germans off Guantanamo, just as Hemingway served in WWI as an ambulance driver on the Italian front and covered major European campaigns for

Collier's magazine during WWII. Island living in Bimini with his boat docked nearby suits Hudson, who enjoys a woman's companionship from time to time but feels no deep regrets once an affair ends, though obligatory parental arrangements over his sons' visits repeatedly put his "ex" in play. His sons' summer visit to the island highlights sun-and-sand frolics, fishing, and water sports, and Hudson's detailed descriptions of each son prove his painterly eye as well as paternal care for his boys. In late afternoons, Thomas Hudson enjoys a "long, pleasantly bitter drink," though a friend feels he "spoils good gin by putting . . . quinine in it."

Like his fictional alter ego, Hemingway would have wished to disentangle from ex-wives, though his sons, like Thomas Hudson's, were much loved: Jack ("Bumby"), born in 1926 to Ernest and Hadley Richardson; Patrick and Gregory, born 1928 and 1931 to Ernest and his second wife, Pauline Pfeiffer. Apart from two months fishing off Havana in 1932, Hemingway's pre-WWII years were spent largely with his family in their French colonial–style Key West house, a gift of Pauline's family, though they sojourned in the US West and in Europe. The year 1933 saw Hemingway on safari in Africa, but his newly customized deep-sea fishing boat, the *Pilar*, brought him to Key West, and in years to come, the *Pilar* was seen docked in Key West or Havana, if not Bimini. (The *Pilar* is now maintained and exhibited by the Cuban government.)

Hemingway's marriages, travels, and war coverage for *Collier's* magazine form an ever-shifting kaleidoscope of the WWII years. An overseas assignment covering the Spanish Civil War introduced him to journalist Martha Gellhorn, and their acquaintance in 1938 prompted his divorce and marriage—his third—to Gellhorn in 1940, after which both

partners reported separately on conflicts in East and South Asia. The year 1941 found Hemingway in Cuba, where the *Pilar* patrolled the waters in search of German submarines, after which he was sent to the European front for *Collier's* at the time of the Normandy invasion. He met journalist Mary Welsh in spring 1944, and by her account, he said to her, "I don't know you, Mary, but I want to marry you. . . . I want to marry you now, and I hope to marry you sometime. Sometime you may want to marry me." Two years later Mary Welsh became the fourth Mrs. Hemingway, having lived with Ernest for months at his farm-like *finca* outside Havana.

Islands in the Stream evolved from a career replete with celebrated titles, from Hemingway's 1926 breakout novel, *The Sun Also Rises*, followed by *A Farewell to Arms*, *Green Hills of Africa*, *To Have and Have Not*, and the critically acknowledged masterpiece *For Whom the Bell Tolls* (1940). His many short stories included "The Snows of Kilimanjaro," and biographer Michael Reynolds voices the conundrum besetting the artist who has achieved the *summa*: "how to make a better one when the last one was the best he could make." Hemingway had not published a book for five years when his 1950 novel *Across the River and into the Trees* was roundly panned, but his reputation was restored with *The Old Man and the Sea*, hailed as "Hemingway at his incomparable best." All the while, he worked on the project that became *Islands in the Stream*, and the posthumous novel pulses with loss for which no remediation is possible.

The life of the serene islander artist, Thomas Hudson, fractures at receipt of the telegram announcing that, following their resplendent summer visit, Hudson's two youngest sons have died in an automobile crash. In a few years, his eldest son will be killed in the war. In the face of such loss, Hudson's life devolves to a *modus operandi* of self-imposed rituals and, finally, to joining a militia in search of German U-boat escapees and a firefight in which he is wounded, apparently fatally.

Careful eating and drinking becomes one of Thomas Hudson's rituals that keep the horrors of his sons' deaths and his existential crisis at bay. Bathing, shaving, and dressing become hyperconscious acts, as do selections from a café. Descriptions of Hudson's snacks, meals, and libations are as detailed in *Islands in the Stream* as Hemingway's famed portrayals of hunting and fishing in his classic fiction. An

accidental food writer, Hemingway could enhance a menu
with mouthwatering specialties lifted from *Islands in the
Stream*, from prawns "cooked in sea water with fresh lime
juice and whole black peppercorns" to a bar's daily "hot free
lunch . . . plates of little hot meat fritters and sandwiches of
French-fried bread with toasted cheese and ham."

The drinks, equally detailed, include the Tom Collins with
coconut water that "tasted of the fresh green lime juice mixed
with the tasteless coconut water that was still so much more
full bodied than any charged water." Thomas Hudson, like
Hemingway, championed the frozen Daiquiris mixed for him at
his favorite Havana restaurant, the Floridita, where the drinks,
as you drank them, sometimes "felt like downhill glacier ski-
ing . . . running through powder snow." At other times, the
same drink "reminded him of the sea": "he looked at the clear
part below the frappéd part of the drink . . . like the wake of
a ship and the clear part was the way the water looked when
the bow cut it." Hemingway's roster of drinkables became so
voluminous that author Philip Greene saw an opportunity for
a biography based on his subject's lifetime of libations. His *To
Have and Have Another: A Hemingway Cocktail Companion*
includes drinks recorded at midcentury in *Islands in the Stream*.

FROZEN DAQUIRI
Ingredients:
1. 2 ounces white rum
2. 1 teaspoon maraschino liqueur
3. 1 teaspoon grapefruit juice
4. ½ ounce fresh lime juice
Directions:
1. Add modest amount chipped or crushed ice to shaker.

2. Add ingredients and shake well.
3. Pour into large cocktail glass and serve.

TOM COLLINS WITH COCONUT WATER
Ingredients
1. 2 ounces Gordon's gin
2. ¾ ounce fresh lime juice
3. 2–4 ounces coconut water
4. 2–3 dashes Angostura bitters
5. Lime wedge

Directions:
1. Add ample ice to shaker.
2. Add all ingredients except lime wedge and shake well.
3. Strain into ice-filled Collins glass.
4. Garnish with lime wedge and serve.

HIGHBALITO *CON AGUA MINERAL*
Ingredients:
1. 2 ounces whiskey
2. 4–6 ounces mineral water

Directions:
1. Fill highball glass with ice cubes.
2. Add whiskey.
3. Fill to top with mineral water, stir gently, and serve.

GIN AND TONIC WITH BITTERS
Ingredients:
1. 2 ounces dry gin
2. 4–6 ounces quinine water
3. 1–2 dashes Angostura bitters
4. Lime wedge

Directions:
1. Fill Collins glass with ice cubes.
2. Add gin.
3. Fill to top with quinine water.
4. Add bitters, stir gently, add lime wedge for garnish, and serve.

RUM SWIZZLE

Ingredients:
1. 1½ ounces rum
2. ½ ounce fresh lime juice
3. ¼ ounce fresh lemon juice
4. 1 teaspoon sugar
5. Dash Angostura bitters
6. 2 ounces seltzer water

Directions:
1. Fill Collins glass with crushed ice.
2. Add all ingredients except seltzer water and stir gently.
3. Add seltzer water, stir gently with swizzle stick, and serve.

GIN AND COCONUT WATER

Ingredients:
1. 2 ounces dry gin
2. 4 ounces chilled coconut water
3. ¼ ounce fresh lime juice
4. 1–2 dashes Angostura bitters

Directions:
1. Fill Collins glass with chipped ice.
2. Add all ingredients, stir gently, and serve. (The drink ought to show a rusty rose color.)

13

GREEN BOOKING

The Negro Motorist Green Book promised "Vacation without Aggravation" in successive editions over a quarter of a century, from 1938 to 1964. A US postal worker, travel writer, and travel agent, Victor H. Green (b. 1892), a WWI veteran, initially began compiling lists of hotels, restaurants, and filling stations that did business with customers of color in and around his Harlem neighborhood. By 1938, he had expanded his listings beyond the New York/New Jersey area and garnered information about facilities in other states. His twenty-one-page first edition listed restaurants and "Hotels in all the large cities East of the Mississippi River" along with tourist homes, roadhouses, dance halls, beauty parlors, night clubs, barber shops, a "School of Beauty Culture," and a "Bootblack Parlor." The guide advertised a taxi service, a valet and dry cleaner, a pharmacy, and Goldman's Wines and Liquors at the corner of Amsterdam Avenue and 155th Street, which readers recognized as Harlem.

"Keep This Guide with You . . . Use It as Your Identification," the newly hatched manual advised, hinting that its pages offered safe passage to alien lands. The fledgling edition included humorous touches ("How to Keep from Growing Old: Always race with locomotives to crossings"), but it also offered a word of caution about "certain sections of the country, where the so-called jim-crow laws are being enforced." The alphabetical directory ranged from Alabama to Virginia, with

"Jim Crow" resounding with every state below the Mason-Dixon Line. Readers were invited to report their experiences and send information to publisher Victor H. Green at 938 Nicholas Avenue, New York City, the home Green shared with his wife, Alma Duke Green.

Guides to lodgings and eateries for US motorists flourished from the pre-WWII years when chain restaurants were unheard of and reliable lodgings a rarity. The American Automobile Association had published its AAA hotel guides since 1917, and a traveling salesman named Duncan Hines (b. 1880) gathered lists of his favorite restaurants for friends before making a career as a food critic by rating restaurants he visited undercover and recommended in *Adventures in Good Eating* (1935), followed by his *Lodging for a Night* (1938), based on his years on the road. Hines never learned to cook, but a spate of recipe books touting his name rolled from publishers for decades. (In 1939, *Adventures in Good*

Cooking and the Art of Carving in the Home, co-authored with his wife, Clara Hines, presented "recipes for home use from Famous Eating Places Throughout America.") Duncan Hines became synonymous with reliable American food, and his name became a licensed national brand for Proctor & Gamble and other companies.

For Black motorists, the *Green Book* became the indispensable brand from its postwar and midcentury editions, 1947 to 1964, all chock-full of locations for lodgings, dining, entertainment, and numerous services. "The white traveler for years has had no difficulty in getting accommodations, but with the Negro it has been different," Victor Green observed in "A Chat with the Editor" in his 1954 iteration. "Now things are different," he insisted. With Green's travel guide, including promotions for air travel at home and abroad, there would be no more "embarrassing situations."

Not so fast. James Baldwin's scorching *The Fire Next Time* (1962) recounts an incident at Chicago's O'Hare Airport bar, where he joined "two Negro acquaintances" to enjoy a few drinks and a bite to eat before their flights. All three men, "well past thirty and looking it," were refused service on the pretext that "we looked too young." Baldwin continues, "It took . . . great insistence and some luck to get the manager, who defended his bartender on the ground that he was 'new' and had not yet, presumably, learned how to distinguish between a Negro boy of twenty and a Negro 'boy' of thirty-seven." "Trembling with rage and frustration," the men were "finally" served, although by that point, "no amount of Scotch would have helped us." Nor did any patron in the crowded bar offer to help.

The *Green Book* did not (and doubtless could not) recommend airport oases among the listings, but nightclubs in the major cities abounded, many with dance floors and music by jazz musicians and vocalists who became legends. The Harlem of New York's Roaring Twenties jazz fame became the tagline for West Coast clubs billing themselves as the "West Coast Apollo," as Curtis Mosby dubbed his "ritzy" Club Alabam located next to the Dunbar Hotel on LA's Central Avenue. "The Harlem of the West," boasted San Francisco's Club Flamingo on Post Street, featuring the "Great Zeke, the prettiest and most comical managing bartender in the West." For Atlantic City, the name was simply: Harlem.

Tantalizing club names beckoned travelers and locals alike. Baltimore's Ubangi and Detroit's Congo tapped customers' African lineage, while other night spots suggested exotic getaways, such as the Shangri-La in Hot Springs, Arkansas, or Club Bali in Washington, DC. The Fiesta drew patrons in Miami, and the Tijuana in Baltimore, where customers might hear Billie Holiday sing or groove to Miles Davis's trumpet, John Coltrane's saxophone, or the Billy Taylor Trio.

Coast to coast, the *Green Book* became a directory of forefront jazz music. Detroit's upscale Flame Show Bar highlighted star women vocalists, including Billie Holiday, Etta James, Dinah Washington, Della Reese, and LaVern Baker, not to mention Joe Turner and B. B. King. On the Gulf coast, a traveler approaching a favorite barbershop for a shave and haircut on LaSalle Street felt perplexed if he had not lived in New Orleans since prewar years, for Frank Painia's barbershop was now a bar and hotel called the Dew Drop Inn. Painia had begun selling refreshments at a nearby housing project and expanded his operation during WWII. Musicians staying at the Dew Drop Inn began to perform in its lounge, and in 1945 the enterprising Painia opened a dancehall. Billed as "New Orleans's swankiest nightclub," the Dew Drop featured topflight jazz and R&B, from Ivory Joe Hunter to the Sweethearts of Rhythm, Clarence "Gatemouth" Brown, the Ravens, Edgar Blanchard, Big Maybelle, and many others.

Reminders of racism recurred from time to time. At the Flame, Black patrons made room for whites from Detroit's affluent suburb of Grosse Point, and no one was arrested for sitting near others of different complexions. Not so at the Dew Drop Inn in November 1952, when white movie actor Zachary Scott and friends looked forward to an evening of drinks and jazz but found themselves arrested along with proprietor Painia. A complaint to the police that "Negroes and whites were being served together" prompted arrests for "disturbing the peace." (The charges were later dropped, though a segregationist law remained on the books for some time.)

All the clubs served profitable drinks, the standard whiskeys, highballs, gin drinks, and cocktails, but bartenders working at the clubs listed in the *Green Book* might not have known of their forebear, the African American Tom Bullock (b. 1872) who presided over libations at the elite Pendennis Club in his native city of Louisville before becoming maestro of the bar at the St. Louis Country Club. Bullock's *The Ideal Bartender*, published before Prohibition, included his specialty juleps and other drinks, and midcentury motorists guided by the *Green Book* might likewise not have known that the drinks they ordered in certain taverns or nightclubs had originated with Bullock, who outlived Victor Green by four years, passing away in 1964. (Green's widow, Alma, became editor of the *Green Book* when her husband died in 1960.) The final edition of 1963–64 opened with an editorial, "Your Rights,

Briefly Speaking!," which credited the "militancy" that civil rights groups "exhibited in sit-ins, kneel-ins, freedom rides, other demonstrations and court battles" for having widened "the areas of public accommodations accessible to all." Victor Green had hoped for the day when his directory might be unnecessary. Tom Bullock would drink to that.

MINT JULEP—KENTUCKY STYLE

Ingredients:
1. 2 ounces bourbon whiskey
2. Sugar lump dissolved in 1 teaspoon water
3. Mint bouquet

Directions:
1. Fill large silver mug with chipped ice.
2. Add dissolved sugar and whiskey.
3. Stir steadily, add mint, and serve.

OVERALL JULEP—ST. LOUIS STYLE

Ingredients:
1. ⅔ wineglass rye whiskey
2. ⅔ wineglass Gordon's gin
3. ½ wineglass grenadine
4. Juice of ½ lemon
5. Juice of ½ lime
6. Club soda

Directions:
1. Fill mixing glass with ice cubes.
2. Add all ingredients except club soda.
3. Stir vigorously.
4. Strain into tall glass containing 3–4 ice cubes.
5. Fill to top with club soda, stir gently, and serve.

IRISH ROSE—COUNTRY CLUB STYLE
Ingredients:
1. 1 ounce grenadine
2. 1½ ounces Bushmills whiskey
3. Seltzer water

Directions:
1. Fill tall glass with cracked ice.
2. Add grenadine and whiskey.
3. Stir gently.
4. Fill to top with seltzer, stir again, and serve.

GIN SOUR—COUNTRY CLUB STYLE
Ingredients:
1. 1½ ounces Old Tom gin
2. ¼ ounce rock-candy syrup
3. Juice of ½ lime
4. Juice of ½ orange
5. 2 dashes pineapple juice

Directions:
1. Fill large mixing glass with ice.
2. Add all ingredients.
3. Stir vigorously, strain into cocktail glass, and serve.

FREE LOVE COCKTAIL—COUNTRY CLUB STYLE
Ingredients:
1. 1½ ounces Old Tom gin
2. 3 dashes anisette
3. ½ egg white
4. ½ ounce fresh cream

Directions:
1. Put ample ice in shaker.
2. Add all ingredients.
3. Shake well, strain into cocktail glass, and serve.

14

ATOMS FOR PEACE

> This weapon . . . must be put into the hands of
> those who will . . . adapt it to the arts of peace.
> —President Dwight D. Eisenhower

President Eisenhower's speech "Atoms for Peace," delivered to the United Nations General Assembly on December 8, 1953, claimed to tip the balance from bombs to the better days just ahead, when peacetime atoms would power electric lights, airplanes, and autos too. The president let others conjure the worldly details while he nodded to the WWII nuclear finale, affirmed the necessity for "swift and resolute" US defense for the foreseeable future, and delivered a high-minded message on atoms for "peace and happiness and well being."

Widespread Atomic Age angst nonetheless worked itself into midcentury poetry, prose, and film as the future seemed to hover between wisdom and mayhem. Eisenhower's three-thousand-word speech boiled down to a five-word catch-phrase: "Wise up or blow up." Poet Allen Ginsberg's *Howl* howled, "America . . . Go **** yourself with your atom bomb," while fellow poet William Carlos Williams imagined "a bomb that has laid / all the world waste." South of the border, Jack Kerouac on-the-road pitied innocent Mexicans who "didn't know that a bomb had come that could crack all our bridges and roads and reduce them to jumbles." John Steinbeck's *Travels* found a Midwest road to be nothing less than an "escape route from the bomb . . . a route designed by fear," while Stanley Kubrick's darkly comic *Dr. Strangelove* (1964) generated nervous laughter from moviegoers entertained by the Cold War comedy of errors between the US and the USSR. Jacqueline Susann's bestselling novel *The Valley of the Dolls* let a character's bad news become a figurative "atom bomb."

Soon enough, soothing and enticing atomic messages flooded midcentury media to lead the country across "a frontier into a region of vastly accelerated progress," according to David Woodbury's *Atoms for Peace* (1958). The popular

science writer taught the general reader the ins and outs of nuclear reactors and reminded Americans that the nuclear-powered US submarine *Nautilus* prowled beneath Arctic ice and that "a cube of uranium the size of a child's building block . . . would run a major city for twenty-four hours." The atom, he promised, would be "woven into the fabric of the nation as completely as the telephone."

Advertisers did their best to make it so. A 1960 *Life* magazine featured a homey nuclear fallout shelter with a TV and carpeting, and diagrams of atoms burgeoned to signal modern life and up-to-date products. Electrons circled nuclei in advertisements of the "Futurized" Raytheon television and the "New Norge Atomic Range." Electric utility companies' long-time corporate cartoon figure Reddy Kilowatt became "Reddy, the Mighty Atom." Corporations promised "long-time benefits" from "Atomic Energy," and a "Tasty Uranium Burger" was grilled for forty-five cents in Salt Lake City. "Atomic cars" were promised, and children sucked Atomic Fire Ball hard candies. Newfound public ease with the atom let novelist Max Shulman use the bomb for schtick in *Rally Round the Flag, Boys!*, in which a crusty old-timer opines that heavy rainfall in Connecticut had come from "them atom bomb explosions that causes all this dang rain."

Shulman's comic bestseller, which pivots on an Army missile installation that rocks a quaint Connecticut suburb, reached movie theaters with Paul Newman and Joanne Woodward in featured roles, serving its audience "daily dosages of alcohol," from bourbon to vodka. None of the characters imbibe Atomic Cocktails, which may have been conjured in years to come in nostalgic tribute to the midcentury moment. The Rocket Man and the Apricot Fission superimpose themselves onto a past that honored "the unleashed new giant which peace must tame."

ROCKET MAN COCKTAIL
Ingredients:
   1. 1 ounce rum
   2. 1½ ounces vodka
   3. ¾ ounce Galliano
   4. ¾ ounce lime juice
   5. 1 sugar cube
   6. 1 cup crushed ice
Directions:
   1. In blender, combine ice, vodka, Galliano, and lime juice.

2. Blend until slushy smooth.
3. Pour mixture into 6- or 8-ounce cocktail glass.
4. Drizzle ¾ ounce rum on top.
5. Pierce sugar cube with small skewer and dip into remaining rum.
6. Carefully light the rum-soaked cube and place atop the cocktail glass to ignite.
7. When flame is extinguished, remove skewer and serve.

APRICOT FISSION COCKTAIL

Ingredients:
1. 2 ounces apricot brandy
2. 1 ounce tangerine juice
3. 1 ounce lemon juice
4. 1½ cups cracked ice
5. 1–2 ounces club soda (chilled)
6. Several ice cubes
7. Mint sprig

Directions:
1. Fill cocktail shaker with cracked ice and add brandy, tangerine juice, and lemon juice.
2. Shake vigorously.
3. Put ice cubes in 10-ounce glass.
4. Strain mixture into glass, add club soda.
5. Stir gently, insert mint sprig, and serve.

ACKNOWLEDGMENTS

Chords of memory resound in major and minor keys in this project, for it tracks this author's own vivid midcentury years, from scrunching under a third-grade desk in a duck-and-cover atomic-bomb drill (the floor felt gritty) to the adult evening in a Playboy Club Living Room sipping Johnny Walker on ice and feeling most sophisticated.

Once again, I am so thankful to literary agent Deirdre Mullane (Mullane Literary) and New York University Press senior editor Clara Platter, who saw possibilities in this the third "drinks-and-culture" project. Following *Gilded Age Cocktails* and *Jazz Age Cocktails*, both Deirdre and Clara enthusiastically green-lighted this opus on drinks and the fads, fashions, and personalities that defined the 1950s–1960s midcentury "Atomic"-era cocktail culture.

Every book enters a conversation already underway, and my numerous sources are the bedrock that makes this project possible. My daughter, Claire, gave carte blanche to raid her PhD dissertation on midcentury bachelor pads, which I have done with pleasure and admiration for the depth of her research and fine writing. Artist Susan Bednarski partnered to produce the superb illustrations that capture the flavor of the period, and *Midcentury Cocktails* owes its sleek cover design to Adam Bohannon and its fine interior to Charles Boyd Hames. Ann Marie Owens reminds us of Fort Lauderdale's fabled Mai-Kai

Restaurant, one of the last survivors of America's first-wave tiki tradition. Once again, Martin Coleman has overseen the project, while Ainee Jeong stepped up as manager, and copyeditor Dan Geist has eagle-eyed the text with crucial queries and suggestions.

The reviewers for this project have done invaluable work, both the anonymous reviewer and the well-established food historians Keith Stavely and Kathleen Fitzgerald. The reports have saved this author from embarrassing glitches and offered substantive recommendations for reframing the argument. The reports have benefitted this project immeasurably. My thanks to one and all!

BIBLIOGRAPHY

Albee, Edward. *Who's Afraid of Virginia Woolf?* 1962. Reprint.
New York: New American Library, 2006.

Baker, Trudy, and Rachel Jones. *Coffee, Tea, or Me?: The
Uninhibited Memoirs of Two Airline Stewardesses.* 1967.
Reprint. New York: Penguin, 2003.

Baldwin, James. *The Fire Next Time.* 1962. Reprint. New York:
Vintage, 1993.

———. *Giovanni's Room.* 1956. Reprint. New York: Vintage,
2013.

Bergeron, Victor Jules. *Trader Vic's Pacific Island Cookbook.*
Garden City, NY: Doubleday, 1968.

Blodgett, Peter J. *Motoring West: Automobile Pioneers, 1900–
1909.* Norman, OK: Arthur H. Clark Co., 2015.

Bren, Paulina. *The Barbizon: The Hotel That Set Women Free.*
New York: Simon & Schuster, 2021.

Brown, Helen Gurley. *Sex and the Single Girl.* 1963. Reprint. New
York: Barnes & Noble, 2003.

Bullock, Tom. *The Ideal Bartender.* 1917. Reprint. www.
ICGtesting.com, n.d.

Cate, Martin, and Rebecca Cate. *Smuggler's Cove: Exotic
Cocktails, Rum, and the Cult of the Tiki.* Berkeley, CA: Ten
Speed Press, 2016.

Charters, Ann. *Kerouac: A Biography.* 1973. Reprint. New York:
St. Martin's, 1974.

———, ed. *The Portable Jack Kerouac*. New York: Penguin, 1995.

Cohen, Lizabeth. *A Consumers' Republic: The Politics of Mass Consumption in Postwar America*. New York: Knopf, 2003.

Curtis, Wayne. *And a Bottle of Rum: A History of the New World in Ten Cocktails*. 2006. Reprint. New York: Broadway Books, 2007.

Davies, Pete. *American Road: The Story of an Epic Transcontinental Journey at the Dawn of the Motor Age*. 2002. Reprint. New York: Henry Holt & Co., 2003.

Didion, Joan. *Let Me Tell You What I Mean*. New York: Knopf, 2018.

———. *South and West*. New York: Vintage, 2018.

Donaldson, Scott. *The Suburban Myth*. New York: Columbia University Press, 1969.

Eliot, T. S. *The Cocktail Party: A Comedy*. New York: Samuel French, Inc., n.d.

Erdgren, Gretchen. *The Playboy Book: Fifty Years*. New York: Taschen, 2007.

Fairchild, John. *Chic Savages: The New Rich, the Old Rich, and the World They Inhabit*. New York: Simon & Schuster, 1989.

Friedan, Betty. *The Feminine Mystique*. 1963. Reprint. New York: Dell, 1984.

Ginsberg, Allen. *Howl and Other Poems*. San Francisco: City Lights Books, 1959.

Gordon, Lois, and Alan Gordon, eds. *The Columbia Chronicles of American Life, 1910–1992*. New York: Columbia University Press, 1995.

Green, Victor H. *The Negro Motorist Green Book*. 1954. Reprint. AboutComics.com, 2019.

Greene, Philip. *To Have and Have Another: A Hemingway Cocktail Companion*. New York: Perigee, 2015.

Hauser, Brooke. *Enter Helen: The Invention of Helen Gurley Brown and the Rise of the Modern Woman*. New York: HarperCollins, 2016.

Hawley, Cameron. *Executive Suite*. Boston: Houghton Mifflin, 1962.

Hemingway, Ernest. *The Garden of Eden*. New York: Charles Scribner's Sons, 1986.

———. *Islands in the Stream*. New York: Charles Scribner's Sons, 1970.

———. *To Have and Have Not*. 1937. Reprint. New York: Scribner, 1996.

Hendrickson, Paul. *Hemingway's Boat: Everything He Loved in Life, and Lost, 1934–1961*. New York: Alfred A. Knopf, 2011.

Heyerdahl, Thor. *Kon-Tiki: Across the Pacific by Raft*. 1949. Reprint. New York: Simon & Schuster, 2009.

Honey, Maureen. *Creating Rosie the Riveter: Class, Gender, and Propaganda during World War II*. Amherst: University of Massachusetts Press, 1984.

Jackson, Kenneth T. *Crabgrass Frontier: The Suburbanization of the United States*. New York: Oxford University Press, 1985.

Jasper, James M. *Restless Nation: Starting Over in America*. Chicago: University of Chicago Press, 2000.

Kerouac, Jack. *On the Road*. 1957. Reprint. New York: Penguin, 2016.

Lawrence, Mary Wells. *A Big Life in Advertising*. New York: Alfred K. Knopf, 2002.

Lepore, Jill. *These Truths: A History of the United States*. New York: W. W. Norton, 2018.

Lewis, Tom. *Divided Highways: Building the Interstate Highways, Transforming American Life*. New York: Viking, 1997.

Lynes, Russell. *Snobs: A Guidebook to Your Friends, Your Enemies, Your Colleagues, and Yourself.* New York: Harper & Brothers, 1950.

Mailer, Norman. *The Deer Park.* 1955. Reprint. New York: Berkeley, 1967.

———. *Mind of an Outlaw: Selected Essays.* New York: Random House, 2013.

Mario, Thomas. *Playboy's New Bar Guide.* New York: Jove, 1954–72.

May, Elaine Tyler. *Homeward Bound: American Families in the Cold War Era.* New York: Basic Books, 1988.

Mead, Shepherd. *How to Succeed in Business without Really Trying.* 1952. Reprint. New York: Simon & Schuster, 1995.

Metalious, Grace. *Peyton Place.* 1956. Reprint. Boston: Northeastern University Press, 1999.

Michener, James A. *Tales of the South Pacific.* 1947. Reprint. New York: Fawcett, 1973.

Mills, C. Wright. *The Power Elite.* New York: Oxford University Press, 1958.

———. *White Collar: The American Middle Class.* 1951. Reprint. New York: Galaxy, 1956.

Ogilvy, David. *Confessions of an Advertising Man.* 1963. Reprint. Harpenden, UK: Southbank Publishing, 1987.

O'Hara, John. *The New York Stories.* New York: Penguin, 2013.

Oshinsky, David. *Bellevue: Three Centuries of Medicine and Mayhem at America's Most Storied Hospital.* 2016. Reprint. New York: Anchor Books, 2017.

Potter, David M. *People of Plenty: Economic Abundance and the America Character.* 1954. Reprint. Chicago: University of Chicago Press, 1958.

Randall, Alice. *Black Bottom Saints.* New York: Amistad, 2020.

Reynolds, Michael. *Hemingway: The 1930s through the Final Years*. New York: W.W. Norton, 1999.

Robertson, Josh. *50 Years of the Playboy Bunny*. San Francisco: Chronicle Books, n.d.

Rothstein, Richard. *The Color of Law: A Forgotten History of How Our Government Segregated America*. 2017. Reprint. New York: Liveright, 2018.

Scott, Kathryn Leigh. *The Bunny Years*. Los Angeles and London: Pomegranate Press, 1998.

Shulman, Max. *Rally Round the Flag, Boys!* Garden City, NY: Doubleday, 1957.

Siegelman, Steve. *Trader Vic's Tiki Party: Cocktails & Food to Share with Friends*. Berkeley, CA: Ten Speed Press, 2005.

Spectorsky, A. C. *The Exurbanites*. Philadelphia and New York: J. B. Lippincott, 1955.

Stafford, Jean. *Collected Stories of Jean Stafford*. Austin: University of Texas Press, 1993.

Steinbeck, John. *Travels with Charley in Search of America*. 1962. Reprint. New York: Penguin, 1997.

Susann, Jacqueline. *Valley of the Dolls*. New York: Grove Press, 1966.

Swift, Earl. *Big Roads: The Untold Story of the Engineers, Visionaries, and Trailblazers Who Created the American Superhighways*. 2011. Reprint. New York: Houghton Mifflin, 2012.

Thompson, Christina. *Sea People: The Puzzle of Polynesia*. New York: HarperCollins, 2019.

Tichi, Cecelia. *Electronic Hearth: Creating an American Television Culture*. New York: Oxford University Press, 1991.

Tichi, Claire. "Bachelors, Domesticity, and Domestic Space in Postwar American Culture, 1945–1960." PhD diss., University of California, Berkeley, 2006.

Tindall, George Brown, and David E. Shi. *America: A Narrative History*. 3rd edition. New York: W. W. Norton, 1992.

Webb, Jeanne. *Hey, Lady! Hey, Waitress! Hey, Miss! Yoo-Hoo, Stewardess!* Bloomington, IN: Archway, 2015.

Wetherell, W. D. *The Man Who Loved Levittown*. New York: Avon, 1985.

Whyte, William H. *The Organization Man*. New York: Simon & Schuster, 1956.

Williams, William Carlos. *The Collected Poems*. 2: 1939–1962. New York: New Directions, 1988.

Wondrich, David. *Imbibe!* 2007. Reprint. New York: Perigree, 2015.

Woodbury, David O. *Atoms for Peace*. New York: Dodd, Mead, 1958.

Yeoward, William. *William Yeoward's American Bar: The World's Most Glamorous Cocktails*. London and New York: Cico Books, 2012.

INDEX OF COCKTAIL RECIPES

Acapulco, 88–89
Aku Aku, 104
Applejack Manhattan, 119
Apricot Fission Cocktail, 147

Bacardi Cocktail, 89
Beachcomber, 90
Blue Hawaiian, 105
Boomerang, 107
Bourbon and Water, 46
Bourbon on the Rocks, 43
Brandy Alexander, 67
Brandy Sour, 118

Carib, 89–90
Celtic Frappé, 67–68
Champagne Cocktail, 125–126
Clover Club Cocktail, 66
Coffee with Applejack, 24
Coffee with Old Grand-Dad
    Whiskey, 24
Cuba Libre, 76

Daiquiri, 36
Dark and Stormy, 92

El Presidente, 90

Fog Cutter, 106–107
Free Love Cocktail—Country
    Club Style, 142
Frozen Daquiri, 132–133

Gibson, 76
Gimlet, 67, 119
Gin and Coconut Water, 134
Gin and Tonic, 56–57
Gin and Tonic with Bitters,
    133–134
Gin Martini, 42
Gin Sour—Country Club
    Style, 142
Grasshopper, 75
Gun Club Punch, 106

Helen Gurley Brown
    Chloroform Cocktails, 117
Heublein Martini on the
    Rocks, 46
Highbalito Con Agua
    Mineral, 133

Irish Coffee, 78–79
Irish Fix, 55
Irish Rose—Country Club
    Style, 142

Jack Daniel's (On the Rocks), 87
Jack Rose, 24–25
Jamaica Elegance, 93

Mai Tai, 102
Manhasset, 54
Manhattan, 34, 125
Margarita, 76–77
Martini, 34–35, 66, 125
Mexican Coffee with Rum
    and Nutmeg, 23
Mint Julep—Kentucky Style,
    141

Negroni, 54–55
New Haven Bar Car Double
    Scotch, 47
New York Sour, 56
Noilly Prat Martini, 54

Ocho Rios, 90–91
Old Fashioned, 35, 77
Outrigger Tiara, 104–105
Overall Julep—St. Louis Style,
    141

Piercingly Cold 8-to-1 Mar-
    tini, 118

Pink Lady, 79
Port Antonio, 91–92
Puerto Rican Pink Lady, 91

Rob Roy, 77
Rocket Man, 146–147
Rum Swizzle, 134
Rye and Ginger Highball, 68

Scotch and Soda, 25, 35
Scotch on the Rocks, 42
Seagram's Seven Crown
    Cocktail, 43
Sidecar, 78
Stinger, 88

Tahitian Punch, 103
Tequila Sour, 92
Tom Collins, 75
Tom Collins with Coconut
    Water, 133
Tonga Punch, 103–104

Virgin Mary, 87–88
Vodka Grand Marnier, 55

Whiskey Highball, 24, 56
Whiskey Sour, 78
White Angel, 124
White Lady, 66
Wine-Spodiodi, 23

Zombie Highball, 102–103

ABOUT THE AUTHOR

CECELIA TICHI is an award-winning author and Professor of English and American Studies Emerita at Vanderbilt University. Her *What Would Mrs. Astor Do?: The Essential Guide to the Manners and Mores of the Gilded Age* set the stage for *Gilded Age Cocktails* and inspires Tichi's new mystery crime fiction series set in the Gilded Age—each with "Gilded" in the title.

Another recent title, *Jazz Age Cocktails*, prompts *Midcentury Cocktails*, each mixing the *History, Lore, and Recipes* that span decades of American spirits.

Cecelia Tichi lives in Nashville, Tennessee, and can be followed on her website: cecebooks.com.